Advance Praise for *Unleashing Human Energy through Culture Change*

"Alan and Don have cut through theory and conjecture to communicate a real-world guide for executives to address the challenges of changing a culture head on. This is a must read for leaders who find themselves handicapped by unproductive culture"
—Sam Reese, Chief Executive Officer, Vistage International

"Your culture activates your people; your people drive your success. Alan and Don use a real-world manufacturing environment to teach us how to develop and use a positive employee-focused workplace culture to unleash employees' energy, activate their engagement, and amplify their performance. They demonstrate how caring, connection, and communication can change even the toughest workplaces into high-performing successes. This is practical wisdom that will benefit every organization and should be the focus of business leaders everywhere."
—Jay Forte, MBA, CPC, ELI-MP, Executive Coach, Author, Consultant and President of The Forte Factor

"While the story Rust and Weinstein share is about the auto industry and GM in particular, it's a far more universal story than that. It's a story that shows the very real impact—on people, on productivity, and on profits—of creating a positive workplace culture. It's a story that more leaders need to know."
—David Friedman, CEO of High Performing Culture, and author of *Fundamentally Different* and *Culture by Design*

"I believe that *Unleashing Human Energy through Culture Change* is an absolutely *must-read* book for managers at every level of the organization, and for anyone involved in serious organizational change. Don Rust and Alan Weinstein provide real-life examples of significant change in an industry that historically resists change and is hierarchal to a fault. Making real change is no easy task but using a philosophy of both thought and action that simply develops mutual faith, trust, and respect among and between management and hourly employees really works. The book is clear and thought-provoking. You'll wonder how Don got away with what he did and be amazed at the long-term impact it had on the employees and the corporation."
—Dennis Gallagher, PhD, President, Dennis Gallagher and Associates

"This book describes Don Rust's lifetime journey at GM and massive organizational successes at the Tonawanda Engine Plant. How Don and his team were able to change the culture at the Plant is instructive for every industry and every leader. His message is simple: treat your teams with trust and respect, engage them in the business, and they will lift your enterprise higher than you could ever expect."

—David Brooks, President (retired) and Director, Unifrax I LLC

"It has been nothing short of amazing to watch a struggling manufacturing operation, and a small Chevrolet dealership, partnering to create two highly competitive and successful businesses. The role of culture change should never be underestimated in its ability to contribute to massive improvements in the quality of work life for the people that do the work. It is the unleashing of human energy that makes possible a drive for new and competitive endeavors in all kinds of businesses."

—Duane Paddock Jr., President & CEO, Paddock Chevrolet

"I wanted to thank Don and Alan for telling the story I had the opportunity to live! I was a mentee of Don's in the early '80s and learned firsthand the leadership style necessary to change cultures so that people get engaged in change. From what I learned from my experience at the Tonawanda Forge and Engine plants, I was able to spend thirty years leading, teaching, and coaching organizations and leaders in culture change. This book delivers a clear message. If you care about employees, listen to them, and engage them, they will care about customers, quality, and doing their best, regardless of industry or functional area. People who are valued and treated with respect will be energized, focused on mission and value, and feel involved and empowered."

—Jim Frost, Former Site Manager-Lockport Operations, GM Harrison

Unleashing

HUMAN ENERGY

through

Culture Change

"*Before Rust came, the plant manager hid behind a locked door. Rust not only flung it open, he mingled with line workers and asked union reps for ideas. It was a rational but radical shift (from) a previous culture, where management made decisions and workers— who often knew a better way—lived with the consequences.*"

—Donn Esmonde, News Columnist,
The Buffalo News, May 2, 2010

Unleashing Human Energy through Culture Change

From a Toxic Culture to a High-Energy,
High-Performance Organization

Donald L. Rust

Plant Manager, General Motors
Tonawanda Engine Plant, Retired

Alan G. Weinstein

Professor Emeritus, Canisius College

Hardcover Edition ISBN: 978-0-692-08620-9
Paperback Edition ISBN: 978-0-692-12909-8

Book Cover & Layout: Summer R. Morris
www.SumoDesignStudio.com

DEDICATION

*"The way to develop the best that is in a man is
by appreciation and encouragement."*

—Charles M. Schwab

This book is dedicated to the many thousands of labor and management employees who spent their careers at the General Motors Tonawanda Engine Plant. It was their unwavering work ethic and contributions that ultimately brought about an amazing trail of successes for the plant—and for GM. It was a new collaboration of the UAW leaders and GM managers that proved once and for all that creating harmony in the workplace is the finest condition possible for the quality of work life that every employee should expect and enjoy. Under those conditions, it is now possible for all the GM employee partners to look forward to getting up on Monday mornings to go to their workplace.

We can complain because rose bushes have thorns,
or rejoice because thorn bushes have roses.

—Abraham Lincoln

The deepest principle of human nature
is the craving to be appreciated.

—William James

TABLE OF CONTENTS

PART FOUR: CHANGING THE EXISTING CULTURE

PART FIVE: SUSTAINING CULTURE CHANGE

FOREWORD

So much has been written about organizational culture that it's hard to keep up. The literature offers differing perspectives, from "it doesn't exist," to "OK, it's real but you can't control it, so just measure performance and culture will take care of itself," to "culture is the one thing that offers every organization a competitive advantage." These different perspectives can be rather confusing. I should know, as I read most of them before writing my own book on the topic, the best-selling *Culture Trumps Everything*. Organizational culture is the one advantage that cannot be bought, sold, traded, borrowed, copied, or stolen. Regardless of industry, it has the potential to be the competitive advantage for every organization.

I had the pleasure of meeting Alan Weinstein several years ago in Buffalo, New York, during a series of speaking engagements I had on the topic of organizational culture. Alan is an organizational psychologist who has had a remarkable ability to balance the demands of an academic career with a successful organizational consulting practice for organizations large and small. Alan greeted me with a big smile, a firm handshake, and a genuine curiosity about my views and experiences regarding the topic of organizational culture. I had the unique pleasure of meeting Don Rust—just this past year—at another speaking engagement on the topic of culture. Don greeted me with enthusiasm, a warm countenance, and a humble appreciation for my having taken the time to read an early draft of their book. I told him, with complete sincerity, "It was absolutely my pleasure."

Although the business management, business development, and business leadership literature are replete with books on organizational culture, *Unleashing Human Energy through Culture Change* is unique. Why? The vast majority of books in this area offer evidence for their assertions based on snippets of organizational culture from a variety of organizations and industries. Even when you do find a true case study in the literature, its story is often told from a third-person perspective, making it more distant or sterile. By contrast, this book is a case study told in the first person. It is rich in the personal trials and challenges that face anyone in a position of leadership throughout his or her career.

Don Rust started as an engineer at General Motors—and went on to become a plant manager at GM's Tonawanda Engine Plant, which was the largest and most efficient engine plant in the world. And it was, in large part, Don's understanding of the power of culture that fueled both his success and the success of the Tonawanda Engine Plant. This book is a firsthand account of how a single person can help build a culture—or, more specifically, a subculture—inside a larger organization and how that subculture can create world-class performance inside that individual's sphere of influence. Don is not a psychologist or consultant, well-versed in the theories and application of organizational culture. He is an engineer who saw problems that needed to be fixed—and fixed them. And he did so by looking beyond what he was taught in engineering school and by assessing the needs of the people who worked for him and with him.

Alan Weinstein brings to the book the structure, broad-based understanding, and accessibility of a successful psychologist working in the field of organizational consulting. He does a masterful job of illuminating the critical insights and implications of the stories from Don and the Tonawanda Engine Plant.

I particularly like the framework of this book. From the very beginning, both authors emphasize that what brought them together to write this book are their shared beliefs around employees. Those beliefs include: 1) faith, or the belief that most employees want to do well where they work; 2) trust, or the belief that employees will want to support the goals of the organization; and 3) respect, or the belief that it is essential to treat people fairly and appreciate their contribution to the organization. Many others may have written about these concepts, but this is the first book I have read that gives a first-person account of what was done and what the outcome was—in the real world. This is not an "if a manager does X, Y will be the outcome" type of book. This is an "I did this, and this is what happened" type of book, complete with all the challenges, setbacks, and victories inherent in real-life experiences.

Two of my favorite sections of the book include the introduction of a new construct, "Industrial Depression," and a "Practical Discussion of Human Energy." In the chapter on Industrial Depression, Don and Alan apply a term that is usually used in clinical psychology ("depression") and apply it, quite aptly, to an industrial organizational setting. What is most compelling is that while reading this chapter, you can imagine being at GM and feeling what those employees were feeling and experiencing what they were experiencing. As for human energy, it is not a topic that is widely discussed outside of literature that is considered "spiritual" in nature. Yet, in their practical discussion of the topic, Don and Alan give you a clear behavioral assessment of what human energy looks like, both when it is present...and when it is absent.

Rather than being abstract or theoretical, this book is unique in its ability to document the steps and experiences of the more than forty-year career of a single person, in a single organization, and how that person applied the concept of culture to improve performance—no matter where he was in the organization. It is also unique because it leverages the knowledge and business acumen of an organizational psychologist with experiences across multiple organizations—and focuses these perspectives on the history of a single organization, as told through the perspective of one long and successful career. In essence, it is a labor of love by both authors, written to remind one organization of how it has achieved greatness in the past—and to shine a light into a dark and uncertain future so that other organizations can achieve a similar greatness. The authors have focused on organizational culture because they both understand that culture has the potential to unleash energy and provide an organization with a tremendous competitive advantage—because culture does, indeed, trump everything.

—Gustavo R. Grodnitzky, PhD
Author, Speaker, Psychologist
President, Gustavo Grodnitzky, PLLC

PREFACE

"The greatest humiliation in life is to work hard on something from which you expect great appreciation, and then fail to get it."

— E. W. Howe

There are many books available that attempt to describe some aspect of how a major corporation, industry, or business recognized the need for change and how they went about it. In some cases, the change had been successful, in terms of financial or some other desired performance measure.

This book will deal with the subject of culture change at the Tonawanda Engine Plant, a major manufacturing operation of General Motors. The authors believe the strategy and principles applied in this book can provide inspiration and guidelines for those willing to invest in major cultural change in their business. The culture change presented in this book is based on actual applications of ideas and initiatives, many of which were successful and a few of which were not.

However, the result was a complete culture change at the GM Tonawanda Engine Plant. What was a hostile environment with low morale and low productivity gradually became one with high energy, high morale, and high productivity. Even more impressive is that this culture change has stood the test of time: more than thirty years have passed, with five plant managers, since this change was initiated. The Tonawanda Engine Plant remains one of the most productive and successful plants within the General Motors Corporation. Over the past few years, GM has invested more than one billion dollars in new machinery and systems at the Tonawanda plant.

We look forward to telling our readers how this change took place and how it is sustained to this day. A brief explanation is in order regarding how we have chosen to tell the story of the cultural change at the Tonawanda Engine Plant.

As authors, we decided to write our book, for the most part, in the first-person plural, using "we" to describe the initiatives and experiences in GM and the Tonawanda Engine Plant. To the reader, this may seem like Don and Alan mutually sharing what we describe throughout the book. However, this is not the case. Almost all the activities and events described in the book were initiated by Don and the managers and workers who worked with him. We considered writing our book in the third person. However, this seemed contrived and distant. In the occasions where we use Don or Alan's name and break from the first-person plural, it just seemed appropriate to fit the situation.

Our choice of "we" underscores our shared belief in the values of faith, trust, and respect for the workers. By faith, we mean the belief that most people are basically good and want to contribute to positive outcomes. By trust, we mean having confidence that people will support an organization and its goals, if treated fairly. By respect, we mean treating people fairly and appreciating their contributions to the goals of an organization. Every individual deserves to be treated as a human and not as an interchangeable tool of management. We share these values as fundamental beliefs that drove the profound changes in the culture that took place in the plants that Don Rust managed throughout his career as a General Motors executive.

This book begins with the origins of GM's culture. We feel it is important for the reader to appreciate how this culture began and how it continued to be reinforced throughout the years. We also felt it important for our readers to understand how and why Don became a change agent when other executives in GM were so indoctrinated into the existing culture. Although we lay the groundwork for culture change in the first nine chapters, our readers who are impatient to learn about culture change at GM may want to skip ahead to Chapter 10.

ACKNOWLEDGMENTS

Several people helped to critique, edit, and prepare this manuscript. Each had an important role in helping us to be clear and accurate in our writing. Two of our reviewers were GM executives who lived through the experience of changing the culture of the Tonawanda Engine Plant.

Don Gray was an industrial engineer and master mechanic at the plant during Don Rust's tenure as plant manager. He made extensive contributions to the accuracy of factory product representations, sourcing of critical components of engines, and design of the plant's bidding processes. His review of our manuscript helped to assure accuracy in recounting the many changes that are described here.

Jim Frost was an electrical engineer and manufacturing manager during Don Rust's tenure as plant manager. He contributed to our understanding of the necessary changes that had to be adopted in the plant's quest for a passion for excellence and quality control processes. His valuable input to the technical process and his broad background in manufacturing were central to the changing culture at the plant. Jim's review of the manuscript helped us to stay true to the changing culture that he participated in creating.

Dennis Gallagher, PhD, is an organizational development expert with vast experience in culture change within large organizations. Dennis not only read the manuscript but offered many insights on how to improve our communication of culture change. His understanding of organizational behavior helped us to clarify the underlying basis of the cultural changes that were implemented at the plant.

Every writer needs an editor to check for meaning, spelling, and clarity. Steve McCabe is an outstanding editor. He scrutinized the manuscript, correcting our mistakes and offering invaluable comments that encouraged us to be clear and concise. With Steve's input, this book is more readable and easier to understand.

The authors are most thankful to Lisa Maloney, who volunteered her time to organize our writing into a manuscript. Her contribution of time, patience, and diligence is greatly appreciated.

Any endeavor such as writing a book requires many hours of thinking, writing, and reviewing, not to mention the many meetings between the authors. We want to thank our wives, Arliss and Tamara, for allowing us the freedom to pursue our passion in writing this book.

—D. Rust and A. Weinstein

PROLOGUE

This is a story that needs to be told.

It is a story about one of the most powerful and successful companies in the world and how it self-destructed, ultimately declaring bankruptcy. The seeds of destruction were apparent even during its most successful years, when it reported strong sales and financial results. In 1965, General Motors owned 60 percent of the U.S. automobile market and was making inroads in other countries. The company's biggest fear at the time was that the government would file an antitrust suit against it and divide it into smaller companies. Those fears were short-lived, as the market share and financial health of General Motors deteriorated over the decades that followed.

This is a story written by two people who witnessed the decline of this great company. Don Rust is a graduate of General Motors Institute (GMI), the university training grounds of GM executives. GMI was to General Motors as West Point is to the U.S. Army. GMI, now known as Kettering University, was a great engineering school with a proven history

1

of turning out great automotive engineers. It was not lack of intellectual or engineering talent that brought down GM. What the company failed to master was how to nurture a culture that would sustain its technical success.

Don Rust began his GM career like most GMI graduates, at the bottom of the management hierarchy. He had to prove himself if he were to advance. He fit the role cut out for him with regard to his talent. But Don was different from many of his GM colleagues in a very fundamental way. From his first assignment, he observed the major fracture between labor and management within the company. What he saw violated his basic values and belief in a better, healthier organization. Management held very negative attitudes toward the United Auto Workers (UAW), and this was manifested in the everyday treatment of union workers. This anti-union attitude was pervasive throughout the GM organization. Don refused to accept the dominant GM culture that permeated every assignment he was given. In the chapters that follow, Don will tell his story about how he was able to change this negative culture into a positive one at several GM plants, culminating in the dramatic turnaround of GM's largest engine plant.

Alan Weinstein is an organizational psychologist who balanced his academic career with an active consulting practice. While in graduate school, Alan did an internship at GM headquarters in Detroit. His impressions led him to choose an academic career over one in industry. The reasons for his choice were clear to him: politics and dysfunction permeated GM headquarters. He saw layers of bureaucracy, top-down autocratic leadership, and a failure by the company to face its own vulnerabilities. A few examples will illustrate Alan's perceptions.

In the mid-1960s, when Ralph Nader wrote his book about the Chevrolet Corvair, *Unsafe at Any Speed*, the response by GM was not to examine the Corvair's safety record and respond to Nader's claims.

Instead, the company's response was to hire a private investigator to gather personal information about the author that could be used to discredit him. Nader sued GM and was awarded enough money to support his not-for-profit organization for years to come. GM's arrogance was indicative of how strongly the company perceived itself as invincible. The company's rallying cry was, "As GM goes, so goes the nation."

In the early 1980s, Alan and his colleague Michael Gent were invited to help the GM Tonawanda plant train its workers for the future. What they observed was a highly dysfunctional company with labor strife and hostile supervision. They witnessed superintendents berating supervisors in public. They heard union leaders openly discussing their distrust of management. One experience that demonstrated the dysfunctionality of management happened after a rare invitation for outsiders like Alan and Michael to lunch in the executive dining room. Instead of a meeting place where executives could talk about their day and enjoy some time off from the stresses of work, the tension in the dining room was so strong that one could hear a pin drop from the silence. It was obvious that things were not right at the Tonawanda Engine Plant.

The two authors of this book formed a team, combining the experiences of a high-level GM executive who observed firsthand the company's dysfunction and culture, and an organizational psychologist who spent his career observing and analyzing organizations, including GM. Together, they offer a multifaceted view of GM's history, its greatness, its decline, and its hope for the future. They will tell the story of how this once-great company self-destructed and how it can regain its greatness—if it has the will to change. The story includes how Don Rust was able to turn a failing engine plant, the largest in GM, into one of GM's most successful engine plants. The lessons learned from Don's success offer hope, not only to GM but to any company willing to transform its culture from one of dysfunction to one where all employees are treated with respect and dignity. It is a story of how a company can bring its internal stakeholders together to work as a team, learning how to improve its product quality, its productivity, and, most importantly, the quality of work life for the people who do the work.

PART ONE:
THE EARLY YEARS

CHAPTER 1

The Early Years of the Auto Industry

The second decade of the twentieth century and into the 1920s and early '30s saw unprecedented growth in the automobile industry. The need for transportation products of all sorts, sizes, and uses was expanding rapidly across the country. The demand for these products was escalating faster than the early factories could produce them. This set in motion the need to escalate production in a labor-intensive industry. Considerable pressure was placed on workers to increase their productivity in a very physically demanding factory environment.

Henry Ford was given credit for inventing the assembly line, a new way to bolt his products together. The assembly line dramatically increased the productivity of Ford plants by reducing the amount of time to manufacture an automobile with fewer workers. It wasn't long before other auto manufacturers would adopt the assembly line concept to produce their products. Ford's 1922 autobiography, *My Life and Work*, described several of the benefits of the assembly line, including the reduction of heavy lifting by workers, the ease of training workers, and the ability to hire immigrants and workers with limited skills. However, as in any radical change, major unanticipated problems soon materialized on assembly lines, such as boredom, repetitive motion injuries, and high employee turnover.

To keep up with the demand for automobiles, factories needed to attract large numbers of workers. These jobs attracted immigrants and poor people from the southern states who were offered the opportunity for a well-paying job in the auto factories up north. This mass hiring of low-skilled workers seemed to satisfy the employment needs of the plants, at least in numbers. However, training poorly educated workers on how to assemble the various components that go into cars while the cars are moving along the assembly line proved to be more daunting than anticipated by the managers who supervised production.

The organization charts for these early plants exhibited the beginning of what would become a rather typical bureaucratic hierarchy. There would be someone at the top, usually called the general manager. Below the general manager were staff and department heads, often referred to as superintendents. The next level was the general foreman, who, in turn, supervised the lowest level of management, the supervisors of the people who actually worked the assembly line. This bureaucratic structure became entrenched and would later turn out to be a bottleneck in making changes to the negative culture that had developed in auto plants.

Even a casual look at this bureaucratic organization chart would lead one to the conclusion that all the authority and control was manifested at the various management levels. No input or representation was visible for the people who were actually doing the work. The industrial culture at the time gave management the opportunities to push and drive the workers unmercifully in the ever-increasing demand for higher and higher production levels. And this they did, ignoring the signs of worker unrest and resentment that were building within the workforce.

Management viewed workers as just numbers in the production process. Workers were often seen as obstacles to ramping up auto production. This led to many instances of worker abuse, with little opportunity for the workers to respond or protect themselves. In most situations where abuse occurred, the psychological damage to a worker was severe but often not readily visible. Workers were without power to resist the incessant demands from management. To make matters worse, the supervisor who practiced tough or abusive behavior toward workers was viewed by management as strong and decisive. These supervisors were given high ratings and opportunities for advancement. A modern definition of this leadership style might be called "bully management." We, as authors, will have more to say about this management style in later chapters of the book.

Despite the internal tensions that were brewing within the auto factories, the growth of auto and truck manufacturing continued through the years up to December 30, 1936. It was on that date that the workers in one of General Motors' plants, the Chevrolet Engine Plant located in Flint, Michigan, demonstrated against the bully management styles that had been allowed to persist over the years. On that date, these Flint workers commenced what was, and still is, referred to within General Motors as the "sit-down strike." All the workers in this Chevrolet plant refused to work until they could obtain some kind of representation and protection from the management. The strike went on for forty-four days of unmitigated accusations and claims of abuse.

During this time, leaders emerged within the workers on strike who took on the role of representatives. These representatives emboldened workers to continue the sit-down strike until worker demands were met. These representatives were the forerunner of what would later become the United Auto Workers Union, better known as the UAW. On the forty-fourth day of the sit-down strike, an agreement was reached. This was a momentous event for the workers. For the first time, they had a voice in how they were to be treated. The UAW was granted the authority to represent all GM auto workers from that day forward.

To this day, the UAW and GM management are still in an adversarial relationship. History has not favored change, and the remnants of the 1937 sit-down strike still linger in GM's culture.

CHAPTER 2

The State of Manufacturing
in the Forties and Fifties

During World War II, automobile manufacturers played an important role in converting their factories to produce the machinery of war, such as tanks, military vehicles, airplanes, and weapons. The production of new automobiles would have to wait until the war was over. After the war, with tens of thousands of soldiers returning home, the demand for automobiles was strong. New automobiles and trucks rolled off the assembly lines. It was not unusual to see customers lined up at the dealerships, just to get a glimpse of the new models that were appearing almost every year. Employment in the auto plants grew substantially as the demand for newer and more luxurious cars hit the markets.

But all was not well in the factories.

DEALING WITH THE UAW

The UAW had gained recognition and strength since the days of the sit-down strike that had taken place in 1936-37. Incessant demands for higher wages, better working conditions, and safer machinery were the norm, and the collective bargaining processes that came with labor contracts was literally endless. The leaders and officers of the unions were elected by the workers, and quite often they were selected because they were perceived as the toughest negotiators. There were far too many work stoppages caused by strikes over the language in the labor contracts or new work demands that were always being made.

At the same time, the auto industry was coming under ever-increasing demand for higher production and better efficiencies while seeking to offer the highest quality for its products. The wedge between management and the unions seemed to be driven ever deeper as the years went by. Management did make some attempts to mollify the union leadership and their workers with a kind of pat-on-the-back approach toward the workers. Management would often stand at the plant gates as the workers entered the plants with signs that read, "Our Workers Are Our Greatest Asset." It sounded good, but to workers, there was still a sharp contrast between these words and the way they felt they were being treated. Workers and their unions continued to exhibit a deep distrust of anyone in management. Many times, events seemed to make clear that management actually loathed its factory workers. Was it any wonder, then, that so little productivity and efficiency could be attained each year? For example, the plant budget, which was never shown to the workers, would often call for an increase in productivity of 1 percent. This increase seemed reasonable, but at year end, it was hardly ever met.

Over the ensuing years, GM and the UAW had settled on what would be a national labor agreement that was supplemented by a local agreement at the individual plant level. Even with this broad agreement, a never-ending battle continued between the negotiating parties at both the national and local levels to get what each side considered an acceptable agreement. It was often very evident that no serious compromising was taking place during these negotiations. Eventually, a potential contract would be hammered together that represented the best deal that each side thought could be sold to the workers. That was followed by a time of explaining the new contract to the workers, who would ultimately cast their votes on whether to accept the new contract.

At times, the contracts were voted down, and a more intense level of negotiations would follow. If a new agreement could not be reached, the union could bring new pressure in the form of taking a strike vote with its members. Over the years, there were too many times when the workers would walk off the job, and that would bring a much higher level of negotiations. Of course, during a strike, GM would lose massive amounts of revenue, money that would never be recovered. In the case of extended strikes, there was always the added factor of sales lost to competitors. Eventually, the negotiators would arrive at a settlement that the workers would ratify. Although the vote indicated acceptance of the contract, it did not bring about peace in the plants. Management would lament the unfairness of the process and the agreement, while the unions would give themselves credit, celebrating their success in extracting more gains.

Unfortunately, this became a ritual that repeated itself every few years, whenever an existing contract was due to expire.

This ritual of protracted negotiations and increasing demands by union leaders on behalf of their workers masked a far deeper underlying problem: what passed for cooperation was really just a tenuous truce between management and the workforce. In reality, workers never got what they really wanted. They wanted respect and recognition, better working conditions, a safer workplace, job security, and a decent wage. What they often got was more money and hard-fought concessions on everything else—but never the recognition and respect they so desperately wanted. In many ways, GM management and the UAW were going through the motions of negotiating, but they never actually tackled the real issues in the plants.

AMERICA'S LOVE AFFAIR WITH CARS

In spite of these uneasy conditions under which GM and the UAW coexisted, both parties deserved credit for the fact that the cars and trucks they produced were surprisingly good for that time in automotive history. They had not yet experienced any serious competition, other than that of other domestic manufacturers that were struggling with the same work issues. The marketing strategy of the auto industry had captured the attention and anticipation of the public and potential customers by announcing new models and designs almost every year. Automakers even enhanced the mystery of their new models by covering them behind a cloth during the delivery period. The dealers would hide the new models somewhere in the showroom until the big day, when the wraps came off and the public was invited to come see what was new. It was a big event and symbolic of the love affair between the automobile and the American car-buying public.

After the earlier years and very public struggles of the auto industry and on into the later 1950s, not much was really known by the public about life in the factories. To the contrary, it was more or less accepted that conditions must be good. The public perception was that the industry paid well and offered good benefits and that an auto industry job was highly desirable. After all, it was very exciting to hold a job in the industry that produced a variety of products that were held in such awe by the American public.

DON RUST MAKES A CAREER CHOICE

It was the lure of the auto industry that attracted Don Rust to pursue his career there. But his entry was delayed a few years by other major events in his life. In 1955, after serving a nineteen-month tour of duty in South Korea during the Korean War, Don returned to the life on the family farm in Minnesota that his military service had interrupted. It was an easy transition from military life back to the farm he was raised on. The farm offered peace and comfort. It also helped Don reunite with and reinforce the values he had learned growing up on the farm. There, he found freedom and work that was highly satisfying. He loved the sense of camaraderie and support that was ingrained in the farming community and the overriding cooperative spirit of farmers who would help each other in every way needed to work their farm and harvest its crops. He loved the values of the farm, particularly the mutual respect farmers held for each other and the strong work ethic that permeated farm life. However, one difficult year of farming convinced Don that another career might be a better long-range plan.

While farming was familiar and Don fit right in, he realized this was not the career he had chosen for himself. In 1956, he decided to leave the life of a farmer and begin attending engineering classes at a local college. At the same time, Don, always fascinated by cars, took a job at a local Buick car dealership. There, the manager of the dealership befriended Don and encouraged him to apply to the General Motors Institute of Engineering in Flint, Michigan. Don applied for and received a scholarship from the Chevrolet Engine Plant in Flint, Michigan, to attend the General Motors Institute. This began Don's forty-year career as an automotive engineer and executive. He had seized the opportunity to embrace his excitement for automobiles, leaving the farming community, where the economic future seemed risky and challenging. He embraced this change with enthusiasm and hope for a rewarding career with GM.

CHAPTER 3

The Origins of a Change Agent

People don't usually think of a farmer as a change agent. But Don's early life experience of growing up on a farm was an important contributor to why he became so passionate about changing working conditions at General Motors. To understand why this was important, consider what farming life was like in Don's upbringing. If you were to ask Don about his early memories about farming, he would talk about the hard work, long hours, fighting with nature, and, of course, close family, hearty meals, and a deep appreciation for human dignity that are all part of farming. He would also tell you that farmers are good people with good values. You will see this theme played out in Don's career as an executive at General Motors.

A close look at the culture of a tightly knit farming community will help reveal what compelled Don to become a change agent. How would a farming background lay the foundation for Don Rust, the farmer, to become Don Rust, the GM manager who created dramatic changes in the plant culture at the GM facilities where he worked and served? To understand how Don became a change agent at GM, it's important to understand the most common challenges that farmers face if they are to succeed as a business. These are the challenges Don lived with as a farmer.

FARMING REQUIRES LONG DAYS, STARTING EARLY AND ENDING LATE

To understand farming, it is helpful to become familiar with its culture. The traditional farm day starts before breakfast. This is necessary to tackle the mandatory chores of caring for livestock, which may include horses, cattle, hogs, sheep, and chickens. If the farm is a dairy farm, the cows must be milked, and the milk must be carefully contained until it can be transported to processing stations. Milk, unlike other farm products, requires that strict sanitation standards must be adhered to, and it takes substantial time out of every day to do it right.

A large and healthy breakfast is for the most part traditional and is eaten before the rest of the day's schedule can take place. The rest of the day, weather permitting, may be spent working in the fields. This work could encompass preparing the land for the planting season. In the earlier years, the soil had to be plowed or disced, and sometimes dragged, to smooth out the surface for actual planting. It was hard and tedious work. The field work would generally end in the late afternoon, allowing time to repeat most of the early morning chores. Finally, the day would conclude with a large evening meal that was commonly referred to as supper.

FARMING CAN BE A RISKY BUSINESS

Farmers are at the mercy of the weather cycle. If there has been any significant amount of rain, the fields cannot be worked until the surface soil has dried. Sometimes, an unusual season of wet weather can delay the spring planting work. Crops such as corn, soybeans, oats, barley, and wheat need a critical time frame for germination and growth in order to ripen for harvest. The weather can raise havoc during this growing period if there are heavy winds, hail, low temperatures, or drought.

The harvest is an especially exciting time for the farmer. It is only then that the return on investment of time and labor can be measured. In the early years of farming, success was measured by how many bushels of corn, soybeans, oats, barley, or wheat were yielded per acre of farmland. A bumper crop of corn would produce something in the neighborhood of fifty bushels per acre. Soybeans had not yet become a measurable product, but oats would produce thirty bushels per acre, and so on. If there were bumper crops, there was substantial satisfaction with the year's accomplishments, and new investments could be planned. The economics of the farm lived or died on the yield at harvest time and the price farmers could get for their crops.

FARMING MUST HAVE PRODUCTIVITY FOR SUCCESS

It is interesting to look back to the earlier years of farming to spot the need for ever more productivity. With the advent of new kinds of machinery, farmers welcomed how they could increase the yields of their crops. Not only did they need good and better yields to produce the food that a hungry world demanded, but there were new demands for their crops in new markets. Starting in about the 1960s, the farm machinery manufacturers became much more aggressive in the design and manufacturing of an ever-changing array of new machinery.

The earliest tractors had metal wheels with heavy lugs to provide the traction to pull heavier and heavier equipment. It was a time of real excitement when the first tractor came to market with inflated rubber tires. These new tractors could be equipped with cultivators that would handle two rows of corn instead of one. That was real productivity improvement. At the same time, corn was being planted in rows, with each hill forty inches apart and typically containing three seed kernels. The close measurement of the forty-inch distance between hills of corn allowed the farmer to cultivate the field lengthwise as well as crosswise. In a normal year, corn would be cultivated four times, to keep the growth of weeds under control and allow more of the ground's moisture to be absorbed by the individual corn plants.

FARMING REQUIRES MAJOR ORGANIZATION TO HARVEST THE CROPS

Later in the summer, the oats, barley, and wheat would reach their ripe stages, and the harvest would begin. The small grains were almost always cut and bound into bundles by a machine that was called, logically, a binder. The binder would deposit the bundles at uniform intervals as the machine proceeded across the fields. The bundles would then be "shocked," or placed with the grain ends up, in stacks of six or eight. This shocking allowed the bundles to dry in preparation for the threshing process.

The neighboring farmers usually gathered together to create a threshing crew. The head of the threshing crew would operate the threshing machine, which separated the grain from the straw. This machine was driven by a long belt from one of the farmers' tractors. The rest of the crew would proceed to the fields of shocks and load the bundles on a wagon with a specially built rack on it. Each rack was piled high with a load of bundles and then towed to the threshing machine either by a team of horses or, later on, by a tractor. The grain was hauled away and stored in a granary located somewhere among the farm buildings.

One of the most memorable events during the threshing days was the noon "farm dinner" that was prepared by the crew's wives and families. It was always a big meal of roast beef, ham, or chicken. Later in the afternoon, a lunch was served for everyone while they continued to work. The typical threshing day was commonly referred to as "the day of five or more meals." No farmer ever forgot the memorable times of the threshing days.

After the small grains were harvested, it was soon time to harvest the corn. In the early days before tractors, it was a huge manual job that took weeks and longer, depending on how many acres of corn had to be picked. The farmer would hitch a team of horses to a special corn wagon and proceed to the field to handpick the corn, one ear at a time. It was not humanly feasible to pick more than one or two wagon loads of corn in the course of a normal day. The eared corn would be transported to another building, logically called a corn crib, for storage. This concluded the harvest season, and it was often followed by plowing the fields for next season's crops.

FARMING REQUIRES PREPARATION AND PLANNING ALL YEAR ROUND

The winter months required more care for livestock because the pastures no longer produced forage after the first frost of the season. The demand for hay was high, and additional corn or grain was necessary to complete the animals' diets. Many of the animals had to be housed in a barn or some kind of outbuilding or shelter during the coldest days and nights. When not caring for the livestock, maintenance and repairs always had to be completed on the machinery to prepare it for the next season.

FARMING DOES NOT INCLUDE DAYS OR WEEKENDS OFF

Farm families were often quite large in those days, and they usually held their neighboring families in high regard. Neighbors often spent time together in the evenings, either with a meal together or just a time of visiting and relaxation. On Saturday night, farm families would often go grocery shopping in a nearby village, and it was one of the highlights of the week. Sunday was still a day of rest in those early days, but the chores still had to be completed every day of the year. After the chores were done, many of the families would travel to a local church of their choice.

THE CULTURE AND SUCCESS OF FARMING

The purpose of this discussion of farming is to offer some insight into the traditional culture that existed within farming as an occupation. It may well have been considered a simple life of living off the land. Unlike today, there were very few, if any, laws and regulations in the 1950s and '60s that could stifle the belief that you could enjoy a successful career as a farmer—but only if you were willing to put in the long days and hard work that were always required.

In looking back on the business of farming and the culture of the people who made it work, it is not surprising that this industry had tremendous success and productivity. Is it any wonder, then, that a young farmer who had been encultured with farm values would enter the world of heavy manufacturing and recognize its major flaws? What this farmer saw was a once innovative company that had in the past offered its employees a good place to work but had now transformed itself into a massive giant with a hostile work environment and a strong anti-worker culture. This farmer learned that it would take years of patience and study to begin to undo the faults so deeply embedded in the GM manufacturing culture.

Is it any wonder, then, that the Japanese auto manufacturers located in rural farm communities to build their U.S. plants? They were well aware of the work ethic and values of farmers and actively recruited these workers into their factories.

The good news is that there is strong evidence that the right kinds of changes in culture can bring about significant improvements.

The remainder of this book will demonstrate how a strong faith and trust in people, and a willingness to take action to change the existing negative culture, would result in an engaged workforce that worked with management, not against it.

CHAPTER 4

Entering the World of Auto Manufacturing

EARLY IMPRESSIONS

t had to be one of the rudest awakenings that a young man just off the farm could face when, for the first time, he walks into this new world called manufacturing. Whatever the beliefs about big industries in general, or what it must look like in that huge plant on Chevrolet Avenue in Flint, Michigan, or how exciting it would be to become a real contributor to something so massive and important, it would be an extraordinary first day on the job.

Students at the General Motors Institute were entered into a cooperative program of working in their sponsoring plant every other month and attending classes at the institute during the intervening months. During their work months, they were assigned to regular jobs in the plant just like the other workers. Some days their work would be on the assembly lines, while other days could be in the machining departments or in the operating support areas. The concept was to give the students a wide variety of jobs and training that was designed to round out their education and prepare them for a future in manufacturing.

Don's first day in the plant started at 6 a.m. His first job on his first day was to lift engine blocks from one roller conveyor to another. It was a grueling job. By lunch break, he could already feel the aches and pains from the strenuous activity. At the end of his shift, he questioned why anyone would give up their friendly farm for a job like this. Don had experienced his share of strenuous farm jobs, but they were not so bad after all when compared with what he experienced on his first day here. But there was no money for a return trip back to Minnesota.

He thought maybe, just maybe, tomorrow would be better.

The end of the work shift was shocking. The whistle blew, and Don saw a stampede of workers heading for the time clock and the nearest exit. He thought, "What was that all about?" The next few days brought things into a clearer perspective: it was increasingly obvious the workers didn't enjoy being there at all. They couldn't wait to leave, and the end of the work shift brought some measure of relief from whatever they had been doing all day.

LASTING IMPRESSIONS

From these early experiences at the Chevrolet plant in Flint, Don came to the conclusion that management had strong negative feelings toward its workers and, all too often, would demonstrate its negativity by the ways it treated them. He would ask himself, "How could a major organization make any reasonable progress under these conditions?" Don thought to himself that the existing culture of the plant needed to change. However, as negative as managers were toward their workers, there was little or no recognition that the day-to-day operating system was holding them back. The dominant attitude was that workers needed to change and that management was only responding to a negative workforce.

This was the beginning of Don's journey through the next forty years of involvement in the automobile manufacturing business. After spending his first twenty-one years on a Minnesota family farm, followed by two years of service in the U.S. Army, the Chevrolet factory was, by contrast, a toxic culture. It was from this perspective that the seeds of culture change were first planted in Don's mind. These seeds germinated and evolved into a career-long search for a new and different kind of operating system in the manufacturing plants where he was assigned.

In the late 1950s, relations between management and the UAW union workers had deteriorated even further. Don found himself right in the middle of a major industrial war, and it had started right in his plant. What was even more disturbing was Don's perception that this war was being fought by workers who were essentially good people but were being treated badly. He felt they deserved much better. They deserved to be treated with respect. As a new member of the operation where five thousand unionized workers were employed, it was very hard to watch how those workers were constantly abused on a daily basis. Lower-level managers were challenged daily to hold the workers to a very strict set of operating rules. It was frowned upon to engage in any attempt to befriend the workers. Lower management was encouraged to penalize workers at the slightest infraction of the work rules. From all outward appearances, it seemed that a "bully management style" was the recommended and accepted way to deal with unionized workers. In some cases, this management style was also used with staff and lower levels of management.

Don knew that conditions were bad, but he did not initially recognize or have a way of describing the severity of the symptoms confronting him. Later in his career, he reflected on his early Chevrolet plant experience as symptomatic of a full-fledged "industrial depression." This is a condition that will be described in greater detail in Chapter 10.

Don worked alongside many workers during his first five years and never once found any evidence that those workers warranted the kind of treatment they were being given. In fact, he observed that most workers did their jobs to the best of their ability while being confronted with a host of difficult conditions set forth by management and their union representatives. It was abundantly clear that most workers did not enjoy any kind of quality in their work life. Their negative attitudes toward management reflected their frustration from working in a toxic organizational culture.

At the end of the journey through the General Motors Institute, most of the students would advance into some part of GM's management structure. There was no misunderstanding that graduates would be expected to abide by the rules of their plant's top management. Lower-level managers were not allowed to make any changes that were contrary to the prevailing rules without first convincing top management of the need for change. To suggest change was perceived as a negative sign that could interfere with one's career advancement. Prevailing norms suggested accepting the status quo and adopting the dominant attitude that workers and their union were the major obstacles to productivity. Only upper management could make changes, and it seemed as entrenched in the same toxic culture as everyone else.

AN OPPORTUNITY TO MANAGE

After five years, graduation from the General Motors Institute took place, and Don entered the field of management at the Chevrolet plant that sponsored his institute education. He received several promotions until he reached the superintendent level. By then, it was clear that the operating system at this plant had been permanently established, and no young manager would be able to change it alone. But in the middle of the 1970s, that suddenly changed, and an opportunity came along for a new job, called traffic manager. Don thanked the plant manager for the opportunity but had to ask a basic question: "What does the traffic manager do?" Little was known about this position because it was housed in a different part of the plant complex. He had never observed the former traffic manager doing anything except sitting in his office chair with his cowboy boots up on his desk.

Don immediately recognized his first chance to revisit the values that had been waiting for an opportunity to surface and help create a positive culture. He was anxious to seize this opportunity to be a positive catalyst for change. He accepted the promotion to traffic manager and could not wait to get started.

PART TWO:
LEARNING ABOUT CHANGE

CHAPTER 5

The Power of Listening

It was 1974 when Don was summoned to the plant manager's office and told he was being selected to be the next traffic manager. This came as a surprise because Don had very little experience with that department. He was aware that the department handled the logistics for the plant, which included the procurement, maintenance, and transportation of material. The Traffic Department also oversaw the fleet of trucks that hauled the castings from the foundry in Saginaw, Michigan, to the manufacturing operations in Flint. Don thought to himself, "The first day on that job should be very interesting indeed." He knew he would have to get up to speed quickly if he expected a smooth transition from his predecessor.

Don knew the plant had a good organization in place, but it wasn't being managed with a great deal of success. The main Traffic Department workforce was involved with trucking operations, and, for some unidentified reason, the truck drivers in this department were intensely disliked by the managers in the rest of the plant. It appeared that some bully management of the truck drivers was occurring, and Don was determined to get an early look at the working conditions of this group.

LEARNING ABOUT HIS NEW DEPARTMENT

The truck fleet consisted of about seventy-five trucks and their drivers. Each truck operated with two trailers in tow and could carry up to eighty tons of castings on each load. It was obvious that the drivers would have to be well-trained to maneuver their trucks safely up and down the Interstate 75 expressway. Don observed that the supervisors of the drivers had been overly aggressive in how they treated the drivers. These supervisors were also known to follow the drivers up and down the highways in unmarked cars for the sole purpose of catching them taking an unscheduled break or rest stop, and issuing a reprimand when they caught them doing so. This cast a pall on the relationship between the drivers and the Traffic Department management.

Soon after accepting the leadership role in the Traffic Department, Don decided to spend some time in the truck garage to learn more about the truck fleet's operations. Without any announcement, he made a visit to the garage during his first week, just to meet supervisors and their drivers. It was a cool atmosphere that greeted him when he walked into the garage. He could sense that the drivers were wondering just what this new, young traffic manager planned to do to make their work lives more miserable than they already were. The visits continued for several weeks before Don sensed some relaxation from the drivers when he was around.

Using what he observed in his many visits, Don created a plan to relieve the tension that existed with the drivers. He had decided that the best way to get to know the drivers would be to invite them to train him to drive one of their trucks. From his years on the farm, Don had a fair amount of experience driving a variety of farm trucks, and he felt this would help break the ice with the drivers.

On his next visit to the garage, Don asked some of the drivers whether any of them would be willing to teach him to drive one of their trucks. There were no volunteers that day. Don was sure they were wondering why he wanted to get involved in driving. They probably suspected he was up to some devious plan to force them to work harder. A few drivers did suggest that they would consider his request and let him know of their decision. Several days later, one of the drivers was waiting for Don when he arrived at his office. After some short greetings, he stated, "You're stuck with me." When Don asked what that meant, the driver stated that the other drivers had asked him to take on the task of driver-trainer, which would start the next morning at 5:30.

When Don walked into the garage the next morning, there was an unmistakable air of anticipation. Everyone wondered what would happen when Don climbed into the cab and sat down in the driver's seat. The truck would have to exit the garage through a rather narrow door, make several quick turns to get onto Chevrolet Avenue, and then proceed uphill to a street that would lead to Interstate 75. The exit went without incident, to Don's great relief, and he and his trainer were soon on the big highway, up to speed. Don had heard the trainer was considered one of the best drivers in the fleet. The trainer said very little but was clearly exercising some close observation of his student. Finally, he asked the question that was undoubtedly on the minds of all the drivers: "So, why do you want to learn to drive one of our trucks?" He also must have observed that Don was a fairly accomplished driver. Don knew that he had better have a good answer. He had to confess that he had truck-driving experience, and he told his trainer his real purpose was just to get to know him and the other drivers so that he could have a better understanding of their work and find out what kind of help he could give them to support them on their jobs.

Following his first day of driving, Don was surprised to learn that other drivers wanted to get involved in the training. Don looked forward to his trips made with a variety of drivers and, while training, getting to know them. Acceptance by the drivers was Don's first break in finding out how to change the bully management he had observed in the garage. He was looking for some fresh ideas on how to relate to drivers. In the back of his mind, Don knew that trust and respect would be the basis of any new efforts to improve the life of the drivers. He was making inroads toward trust and respect by driving with them and getting to know them. Both he and the drivers were enjoying the experience. Don knew that better relationships would be the basis for allowing some of the hostilities between company management and the unionized drivers to finally start to fade.

LISTENING AND MAKING CHANGES

The next big opportunity for Don to change the bully management structure within the Traffic Department came along with the decision to replace all the tractors that pulled the double-bottom trailers that hauled product from Saginaw to their next destination. The old tractors were built by Chevrolet, of course, and the new ones would also be Chevrolets. The department managers made out the orders. The new tractors would be almost identical to the old ones, with the exception of any creature comforts for the drivers. After Don reviewed the orders, he realized the new trucks would not go over well with the drivers. He asked the supervisors to gather a group of the drivers to review the orders and make suggestions on how the trucks should be equipped. As expected, this did not go over well with the department managers or supervisors, but they called the meeting as asked, and the drivers were pleased to attend the meeting.

After reviewing the orders, the drivers stated that the trucks would be fine mechanically. They knew that no mechanical changes could be made in the orders at that time. However, they suggested several options that would have been nice to have for drivers. When asked to offer more justification about those options, they explained that the temperature in the cabs gets up to 120 degrees in the summer. This causes driver drowsiness, which can be a safety problem. Air-conditioning would be a welcome addition, they said.

The second option they were about to suggest created laughter in the room. Don assured them that he would consider their ideas anyway and encouraged them to go ahead. They pointed out that in their daily travels, they often mingled with drivers from other companies, and these drivers would always comment on how cheap the trucks were that Chevrolet provided. The Chevrolet trucks didn't even have air horns on them, the other drivers said. Don expressed surprise at that observation, but he knew that air horns were an important option from a trucker's point of view.

Don asked the drivers to wait when the meeting was over. He wanted to let them know that their ideas were appreciated and their suggestions and ideas were heard. He told them that their concern for safety was well-placed, and the new trucks would all be equipped with air-conditioning. He then directed the supervisors to find the biggest chrome air horns available on the market and make sure all the trucks would have them placed on the trucks for all to see. His decision, as he explained it to them, was that Chevrolet was in the truck manufacturing business. Therefore, Chevrolet trucks should be the best-looking trucks on the highway. Only Don's imagination could conjure up what kind of euphoria these decisions had made when the drivers returned to the garage and learned about what they had accomplished by expressing their needs.

If Don ever had doubts about the impact of the power of listening to employees and making changes, those doubts were rapidly vanishing. These changes were not made as a feel-good management strategy; they were much more than that. Don realized that his employees needed to be engaged and aligned with management. They needed an organizational culture change from the old way of doing business, which had always treated them as pawns in a management-controlled system. They needed a culture change from one that ignored their input to a system that appreciated it and aligned their needs with the goals of the organization.

After the new trucks arrived, more changes were made. All the trucks were repainted with a sharp red, white, and blue paint scheme. Those trucks drew lots of attention out on the highways. Drivers seemed happy and proud of their trucks. They were no longer teased about how bad their trucks looked.

USING COMPETITION TO RAISE MORALE

If there was any doubt about the positive effect of the changes made within the Traffic Department, it was eliminated by way of a competition. The company learned that a national safe-driving campaign was coming. Don and his managers conferred with union leaders and drivers about participating in the campaign. The decision was made to enter into that campaign. When the campaign ended, the Flint Chevrolet drivers came in first. They won with a record of ten million miles logged without a single accident and were awarded the certificate on the following page.

This was a crowning achievement from the same group of drivers who not long before had been bullied, were resistant to change, and had been embarrassed to be seen driving trucks that had been the laughingstock of their trade. This achievement even inspired one of the mechanics to write the poem on the following page. It is testimony to the commitment and pride of the workers in the Traffic Department.

Reflecting on his experiences in the Traffic Department cemented in Don's mind the importance of listening to and paying attention to the people who do the work. He had found his niche in managing people. The results of this management approach in the Traffic Department led to a significant change in productivity and a source of pride among workers. The drivers, with no pressure from management, began making more round trips to Saginaw.

Don saw how the change in the way workers were managed led to a more exciting and interesting workplace. This had, in its own way, created a new level of energy that had never been experienced. From this experience, Don learned that there is a huge reservoir of energy that exists in most workforces that never gets released. This energy only gets released when there is alignment between workers and management, and this alignment requires a strong sense of purpose, or mutually accepted goals. This kind of energy release cannot be demanded of the workers by management. Instead, it is a personal response on the part of the worker, brought about by a culture that supports both the goals of the worker and the company. For the company, the goal is high productivity and worker cooperation. For the worker, the goal is inclusion, respect, job security, and a sense of personal accomplishment. The alignment created between management and workers in the Traffic Department accomplished both. This alignment will be explored further in later chapters.

OUR TRAFFIC DEPARTMENT

The drivers, mechanics, parts men and clerks,
Foremen, dispatchers and others in the works,
Flint Chevy has done it, from the top man on down.
Our Traffic Department is wearing a crown.

With little straight sixes they pulled a great weight,
'Till one day pulled more with the mighty V-8.
And now with big diesels they scream and they roar,
Pulling loads that are bigger and weigh even more.

No accidents! was our goal and our aim,
And the few that did happen were the other guy's blame.
With semis and doubles, big boxes and sleds,
They hauled cases and cranks and cylinder heads.

Mile after mile they rolled over the roads,
Hauling some of the heaviest and diverse of loads.
The Michigan weather is often a test,
But wheels kept on turning, North, East, South and West.

On the first of the fifth month in seventy-five,
The great motto stood - "Bring 'em all back alive."
Credit must go to the bunch with big smiles,
For over the years they've gone ten million miles.

To the old timers, some now out of our ranks,
And to the young upstarts, the department says, "thanks."
With teamwork and effort, our engines which roar,
Our traffic will roll easy, ten million miles more.

Cliff Booth
Mechanic
Traffic Department

CHAPTER 6

Going the Extra Mile

It seemed like there was unfinished business in the Traffic Department at the Flint plant when, without expecting it, Don was promoted to general superintendent of manufacturing at the Saginaw Engine Plant in Saginaw, Michigan. This was the smallest of GM's engine plants, and it would present a whole new set of opportunities and challenges for Don. It did not take long for Don to see the challenges he faced at this new location. The fracture in relations between management and labor in Saginaw was quite visible. Don quickly observed that the Saginaw plant had many unhappy workers, much as he had found when he first arrived at the Flint Engine Plant, and their unhappiness, he learned, was mostly for many of the same reasons he had seen in Flint.

At the time, Don did not realize that he was on a one-year assignment to the Saginaw plant. Historically, Saginaw had always been a place for new general superintendents to grow into the new challenges that would confront younger managers at GM. This gave them the opportunity to move up, with career planning preset by Chevrolet's personnel department. His new brief assignment in Saginaw did not prevent Don from exploring further initiatives in creating change in management styles. His recent experience in the Traffic Department in Flint gave him confidence that his approach to workers was the key to improving results for both the worker and the company.

The workers at the Saginaw plant were somewhat different from those Don had been used to at the Flint plant: they were more reticent about communicating. They seemed to be less willing to enter into conversations about their jobs, or other plant conditions, that might in any way complicate their quality of work life. This condition may have been the result of the frequent management changes that had taken place in the plant. Different managers brought different demands and changes that introduced disruptions and unnecessary turmoil in day-to-day operations. As a result, there seemed to be a noticeable, negative impact on the workers' quality of work life.

CONFRONTING A NATURAL DISASTER

Don's transfer to the Saginaw plant did not require him to move himself and his family. The two plants were only sixty miles apart, so Don decided to commute rather than move. That plan went well enough, but then the winter weather came along. On one occasion shortly after his transfer to Saginaw, a very severe ice storm had taken place overnight, and his drive to Saginaw was difficult.

Upon arrival at the plant, Don expected that more workers than usual might well be absent, but what he found was that only one worker had shown up for work. The storm had been more severe in the Saginaw area, with a major loss of electricity in the whole area. Many of the workers were at home trying to protect their families and finding ways to keep warm. On top of that, there had been a heavy rain before the ice formed, and that had caused many of the workers' basements to become flooded. This made the workers' situations even worse. Weather conditions did not improve the next day, and there was little success in getting the power restored. By then, things were getting desperate at the plant. If the plant were not able to ship engines to its customer plants, those plants would not be able to keep their assembly lines running, losing valuable production time.

What could the Saginaw plant do to avoid this?

SHOWING COMPASSION FOR WORKERS

Late in the afternoon of the second day, several skilled trades' workers had made it to the plant. Don was able to sit down with them as a group to discuss what course of action the plant could take. It became apparent that the flooded basements were the main reason that workers were not showing up at the plant. A plan began to take place. Don suggested calling his former colleagues at the Flint plant to find out whether they had some gasoline-powered water pumps that the Saginaw plant might borrow for a few days. Fortunately, they did have pumps available for loan. Don asked several millwrights to drive a plant truck down to Flint and bring back as many pumps as that plant could spare. The truck returned late that afternoon with eight pumps. By then, several of the union officers were at the plant. Don asked them to take on the task of finding out which workers were the most impacted by flooded basements and to deliver the pumps to those most in need. The first pump was delivered to the plant doctor and then to the workers most needed to get the plant back into operation. The plan worked. The crew delivering the pumps worked day and night pumping basements. Workers began showing up at the plant, and before long it was possible to start the engine assembly line at a reduced speed. By the fifth day, most workers could return to work, and the line was back to normal speed.

When the crisis was over, there was still some concern. The Saginaw plant manager was not so sure Don and his crew had done the right thing by sending workers out to other workers' homes to offer them help with their flooded basements. However, this did not diminish the personal satisfaction the workers felt in helping their distressed workmates. Moreover, workers had experienced a concern for their well-being from management that they were not accustomed to experiencing. In any business, when compassion and concern for worker health and safety are demonstrated, as was the case in the Saginaw plant, the bond of trust between management and worker will be strengthened. This opens a new opportunity for cooperation and collaboration, a foundation for both parties to work together on organizational challenges and opportunities.

A SHOW OF APPRECIATION

Not long after the ice storm problems were solved, the union officers all came to Don's office to talk. Don thought to himself, "The next problem for the plant must be happening." He was floored at what happened next. The officers stated that they and the workers they represented had so appreciated Don's willingness to help them during the ice storm that they wanted to show him the extent of their appreciation. The officers placed a box on his desk and told him to open it at his leisure.

After they left, Don was anxious to see what was in the box. What he found in the box was a case of top-shelf whiskey. Don was not a whiskey drinker, but there was a more perplexing problem. What should he do with this box of whiskey? Having alcohol in the plant was a violation of GM's operating rules against having any alcoholic beverage in any GM building. Right at that moment, Don wondered what might happen if his plant manager showed up at his door. Could this jeopardize his career at GM? Don's first thought of what to do next was to try to get to his plant manager's office before the plant manager showed up at his office.

Don called his plant manager and told him he had a minor problem. The plant manager asked what it was. Don told him, as casually as he could, that he had a case of whiskey under his office desk, where he had hidden it. His plant manager reacted as Don had expected and read the riot act to him about the importance of abiding by GM's rules of order. When the plant manager was finished reprimanding him, Don asked if he might bring the whiskey to his manager's office until the problem could be resolved. Don got a resounding rejection of that idea, so he stated that the box would be out of the plant by the end of the first shift.

It is interesting to analyze the plant manager's reaction. His fear of what could happen if it became known that a case of whiskey was in the plant superseded what had just been accomplished in creating a collaborative relationship with workers. The attention was clearly on the rules and not the opportunity to work together. Any humor or irony that could have been interpreted was lost. We believe this to be a result of the hostile culture that was pervasive within GM, bringing a rigidity to situations like this.

Don dutifully removed the box from the plant. And, to this day, nobody knows just where the box of whiskey went. But Don was sure that some over-the-road trucker was surprised when he unloaded his truck.

In retrospect, this unanticipated situation with weather-related operating problems reinforced Don's theory that showing concern for the workers, and treating them with trust and respect, is always the right way to manage.

MORE CHANGES

The rest of the year was peaceful and promising at the Saginaw plant. Don and his supervisors were able to make some significant engineering changes that helped the plant as well as the workers. One particular change involved a truck gearshift lever for an on-the-floor transmission that was produced in the Saginaw plant. The gearshift lever was tapered from the shift knob down to the end that entered into the top of the transmission. The tapering of the lever was accomplished with a swaging machine that literally hammered the cold steel shaft into its tapered design. To do so created an enormous noise, so loud that it had to be done in a separate brick building, away from everything else. It was unbearable for any worker to spend much time on that job, even with the best hearing protection available. Don was able to get the gearshift lever redesigned by GM engineers. This eliminated the swaging operation entirely, which was a great relief to the workers who had operated the swaging machine. It was another step in the right direction of culture change to see the workers at the Saginaw plant respond to management's attempts at providing a better and more comfortable work environment. It was also well received by workers to be treated well by management—not just occasionally but every day and all day.

One year after his assignment in Saginaw, Don was told he was being transferred to the Tonawanda, New York, engine plant, just outside of Buffalo, New York. He was about to enter a very different work environment, one that would challenge him for the remainder of his career at GM.

CHAPTER 7

I Came, I Saw, I Knew We Were in Trouble

SHUFFLING OFF TO BUFFALO

It was December of 1976 when Don got word from GM headquarters that he was being transferred from the Saginaw Engine Plant in Saginaw, Michigan, to the Tonawanda Engine Plant near Buffalo, New York. No stranger to snow, Don had heard that there were some horrendous winter snowstorms around Buffalo. This weather would be a challenge for him and his family. But he was anxious to leave Saginaw. Not that he had any choice: at GM, when you were offered a transfer, you accepted. That was the GM way. To refuse a transfer was a death wish to your career at GM.

Don was actually excited about this move. He was leaving the smallest of GM's engine plants and moving to its largest engine plant. And Tonawanda was unique, having both a forging plant and a foundry within the same complex. The plant was considered one of the most successful of the twelve engine plants that GM operated. Over the years, Don had hoped that someday he would get a chance to be assigned there.

In December of 1976, his wish came true.

EARLY IMPRESSIONS OF GM TONAWANDA

The Tonawanda plant had a long-standing reputation for producing a variety of engines for cars, trucks, boats, and some aftermarket stationary power applications. To be clear, some of these engine designs were flawed or did not create a strong demand in the marketplace. Among these failures were the Vega and Corvair engines. Each of these had been a new engine design. The Vega engine involved the production of a new aluminum cylinder case bolted onto a cast iron cylinder head. GM misjudged the metallurgical difficulty of bolting these two materials together, and this caused major problems for the vehicles they were designed for. The Corvair engine was an air-cooled, horizontally opposed six-cylinder design. The plan was to install it in the rear of the Corvair. Both vehicles were marketing failures for very different reasons. While not the fault of the Tonawanda plant, these design failures had an impact on the reputation of the plant and the new engines that would be assigned to it.

When you get transferred to another plant in GM, it is customary to lie low at first. After twenty years at GM, having worked in a variety of management positions, Don was well aware of how important it was to get off to a good start. If he slipped and alienated people, it could take months to recover—if recovery was possible at all. Everyone in the plant knew that a new general superintendent was arriving. They were curious about who this guy was. It was not difficult for the people there to check their sources at other plants where Don had worked to glean some knowledge about him, good and bad. Workers, in particular, wanted to know what to expect out of Don. The union had its network, too. It didn't take long for the union representatives to size up the new guy. Don knew they would form opinions about him and his management style before he even arrived.

The Tonawanda plant had three general superintendents, and Don was replacing one of them. His predecessor had not enjoyed a positive reputation. He was shipped out to another GM plant, in Michigan. Don soon learned that his job would be taking over the second shift. Each general superintendent had several superintendents reporting to him. All three general superintendents reported to the plant manager. What impressed Don was the competition among the shifts. Each shift was responsible for getting engines out the door, and, of course, the more the better. The yardstick that measured this was known simply as "The Count." It was clear that the first shift was outproducing the second shift by a wide margin. Management blamed the general superintendent, whom Don was replacing, for the low output of engines on the second shift. It was pretty vicious.

There were two general superintendents on the first shift. One had a traditional style of leadership, meaning he made demands without explanation and expected everyone to follow them. His counterpart on the first shift was thought to be one of the best managers in the business. Don looked forward to working with him.

When the day came for taking over the second shift, Don was faced with an immediate challenge from the plant manager. The first shift was outperforming the second shift, and he wanted that problem solved as soon as possible. Like Don, the plant manager was a graduate of General Motors Institute, and he had a long career at the Tonawanda plant. He was a legend at the plant with a broad knowledge of all operations. Don felt it a privilege to work for him.

Within the first few days, it became clear that there were multiple problems causing the difference in production between the two shifts. First and foremost was the unhappy workforce that sapped much of the energy out of the shift. The workers had been asking for a host of mostly small improvements at their work stations. Management had failed to follow up on these requests, which led to negative feelings toward management. From Don's experience in GM plants in Flint and Saginaw, he knew that production would not improve as long as the workforce issues were outstanding. He named this problem "industrial depression," a condition we will elaborate on in Chapter 10.

AVERTING A MAJOR CRISIS

Don had the good fortune to meet Frank Cantafio in the early days of his assignment on the second shift. Frank was a big man who carried his weight well when it came to representing union members. He was chairman of the Shop Committee and knew his job and his people well. He respected his workers, and they in turn respected him. What followed was a major breakthrough for Don and the second shift.

It is quite likely that Frank saw Don as green. After all, Don was new on the job and to the Tonawanda plant. Frank must have done some research on Don from his contacts in Flint and Saginaw. Frank took a risk and approached Don in a hesitant but friendly way.

Here is how they met.

From his office at the front of the manufacturing floor, Don saw Frank standing outside his door. Sensing that he might want to talk, Don went out and greeted Frank. After some general conversation, Frank asked whether Don knew that union reps were not allowed to enter the offices to talk to management, and he wondered what Don thought about that. Don knew it was a loaded question, and he suspected that Frank was testing him on this rule. Don gave himself a moment to compose his response, looked Frank straight in the eye, and said, "Frank, as long as I am here and whenever you need to talk with me, let's do our talking in my office where we can have some privacy." Frank looked pleased, and Don knew that they had just broken the invisible barrier that fueled the strong negativity between the union and management. This event led to a growing relationship between Frank and Don that would have a major impact—not only on the second shift but on the plant as a whole.

During Don's first few days on the second shift, one of the first shift assembly line superintendents, on his own authority, decided that the best way to improve the production on the second shift was to speed up the assembly line. Without telling anyone about his plan, he did just that. As expected, the workers knew immediately what had happened and called their union representative in to complain. Shortly after, the union wrote up fifty speed-up grievances and presented them to the plant manager. These grievances were written complaints that required a formal resolution by management and union officers. In this case, there was a clause in the labor contract that pertained to assembly-line speed, and the union claimed management had violated this clause. The plant manager was not pleased because workers visibly withdrew their efforts and cooperation in protest of the speed-up.

It wasn't long before Frank came to see Don about the grievances. Don invited Frank into his office, which very likely produced some stares and raised eyebrows from managers who witnessed this breaking of the rules. Don asked Frank what he thought needed to be done about the speed-up. Frank suggested that he and Don go for a walk through the plant, stopping to talk with workers who had problems and had filed grievances.

During their tour, Frank stopped at many of the jobs on the floor, showing Don problems that needed to be fixed. Don listened carefully. Most of the changes were simple fixes like a better work platform, better lighting, or better containers for the supply of parts that were being assembled. Don assured Frank that he could expect each problem to be corrected before the next shift. When Don returned to his office, he gave direction for each problem to be addressed and resolved. This must have surprised Frank because he came by the next day and again asked Don to walk through the plant with him. He proceeded to show Don more problems. Again, by the next day, these problems were taken care of. Frank must have taken a liking to Don because he kept coming to his office, and each time he came, they walked through a different area of the plant, identifying problems that needed fixing. None of these problems were difficult to fix; they just required attention and follow-through.

Not all was well with the plant manager and the other two general superintendents. They were very concerned about the possibility that the fifty grievances could lead to a strike, which would be disastrous by reducing the output of engines and causing customer plants to have to shut down the assembly of cars and trucks. The plant manager and other general managers appeared to lack confidence in Don's readiness to handle such a hot situation so early on his assignment to the second shift.

On one of his visits, Frank asked Don how things were going. Don told him of management's concerns about the fifty speed-up grievances. Don asked Frank if he thought it was helpful that they had gone out to walk together through the problem areas of the plant and that he had seen that the changes that workers had asked for had been made. Frank stated that the workers were more than pleased that Don had personally gotten involved in listening to their concerns and was taking an active role in making the changes they had asked for.

Knowing that the fifty grievances filed could lead to a strike, the plant manager assigned Don Gray, an industrial engineer, to readjust the assembly line speed. Once the line speed was adjusted, Don Rust asked Frank what he thought should be done about trying to settle the grievances. Frank said that in his opinion things were going much better on the assembly line. Much to Don's surprise, and probably as a result of the changes Don was able to make at many of the work stations, all fifty grievances were dropped without prejudice, and the possibility of a strike was averted. Later, Don learned that it was Frank who had recommended that all fifty grievances be withdrawn without prejudice.

It is not clear exactly why it happened, but there was a sense of eased tension on the second shift. There was also a renewed energy on the lines of the second shift. Productivity increased and, in the second week of Don's leadership, the second shift overtook The Count from the first shift in engines produced. Not only was a labor disaster avoided, but the workers stepped up and produced more engines. Frank actually made a statement complimenting Don for his cooperation with the union. This was unprecedented at the Tonawanda Engine Plant. Frank and Don never did try to explain what they had done to bring about such a quick change on the second shift. But Don knew that the success was a direct result of the cooperation between Frank and him. Frank guided Don to the root of the labor unrest, and Don was able to demonstrate not only a willingness to see it but also demonstrate management's concern and commitment to make the changes that directly affected workers at their work stations.

LESSONS LEARNED

There were significant lessons learned from Don's experience with Frank and the union members. As a manager, he did what he thought he was supposed to do. He listened to the workers, removed obstacles that were interfering with the work environment, and developed a cooperative relationship with the union representative. The result was an easing of tension, removal of all speed-up grievances, a renewed energy in the plant, and increased production.

CHAPTER 8

Winning over Hard Hats

Don's assignment at the Tonawanda Engine Plant had gone quite well for the first two years, but that, too, was about to end: he was being transferred to the neighboring Tonawanda Forge Plant, which was a part of GM's massive Tonawanda complex. His experience in the field of steel forgings was somewhat limited to whatever he had learned about that process while a student at General Motors Institute, but he was eager to have a new experience on his résumé.

A CHALLENGING WORK ENVIRONMENT

The workers at the Tonawanda Forge Plant were definitely unlike any others he had encountered at GM, and it didn't take long for Don to find out they were very tough and could put in long days of very heavy work. It was a more dangerous kind of work than Don had observed in the engine plants because it involved heating chunks of red-hot metal to be placed into dies and then forged into whatever parts needed to be formed. The work was both physically demanding and mentally taxing for the workers and required strict adherence to preset safe operating rules. Don needed to get up to speed in a hurry to oversee all the operations these workers were performing.

The machinery in the forging operation was very different from what he was used to in the engine machining operations he had seen in the Flint, Saginaw, and Tonawanda plants. The equipment in this plant was out of date and lacked technical advances that were needed for efficient operations. Realizing this, Don began looking for state-of-the-art forging equipment, focusing specifically on a very advanced kind of machine called a "hotformer." The Swiss had developed the machine and did the early testing of it. Don flew to Switzerland to visit a company named Hatebur, the leader in hotforming technology. Hatebur was very forthcoming with a great deal of information to back up its designs. It was abundantly clear that this hotformer machine exhibited great potential for higher productivity, as well as more accurate control of product quality. Don ordered this machine, which took a year before it was delivered, for the forge plant. This was unusual because most of GM's machines were produced in the U.S.

In order to take advantage of this new machine's productivity potential, it would be necessary to heat the bar stock rapidly as it was fed into the machine's forming dies. That called for more research into what the market had available in terms of rapid-heating potential. It soon appeared that the best steel-bar heater on the market was produced in Wales. Determined to upgrade the plant, Don found himself on a plane to Great Britain. Their bar heater looked good and had full potential to supplement the new hotformer.

The Hatebur hotformer machine arrived and was installed with the new bar heater, which could heat bars to more than 1,800 degrees Fahrenheit in a matter of seconds. The hotformer made it possible to cut the bars into the correctly sized pieces appropriate for the machine that was set up to forge. The productivity of the Hatebur machine was phenomenal, and forging quality was excellent. Everyone was very excited to learn about the success of the new equipment from overseas. No longer would the operators be exposed to the hot metal while removing the hot products from the dies. Instead, the hot metal products were automatically ejected into the waiting bins.

This new process was so successful that an executive at GM ordered three more of the hotforming machines—but ones produced by a domestic machine-maker that was selected against Don's recommendation. Don did not recommend this hotformer because his research had determined the frame of the machine would crack under the enormous pressure of the forging operation. Indeed, the machines did crack and required welded reinforcements to be added into their frames. This repair was a setback, but these hotformers functioned after they were repaired, albeit less effectively than the Hatebur machine. Combined, these four machines in GM's forging processes gave the Tonawanda Forge Plant a significant competitive advantage, allowing it to take part in a major study of GM's forging capacities. The study revealed that Chevrolet could expand the Tonawanda Forge Plant by consolidating the forging operations from three other plants. It was a major move forward for Chevrolet and GM that made them significantly more competitive in the steel forging business.

ACCEPTING CHANGE

The workers at the Tonawanda Forge Plant were receptive to the equipment changes that had been made. They were also receptive to the supportive culture that Don and his management team created. The macho toughness shown by the first shift supervisors gave way to a more supportive treatment characterized by trust and respect. It was obvious that the relationship among workers, union leaders, and

Don's management team had markedly improved. Just as he had seen with changes he had made in earlier assignments, the forge plant workers experienced an improvement in their quality of work life, and a comparable improvement followed in the overall plant performance. The Tonawanda Forge Plant was a real test of whether a culture change could be successfully undertaken in this very different kind of manufacturing operation. There was little doubt by anyone working in this plant that the many changes made by management were the reason behind its success.

As a result of his success in the five years he had run the forge plant, Chevrolet transferred Don back to the Tonawanda Engine Plant, but this time as the plant manager. Don could hardly wait to get there and rejoin what he would later describe as the finest workforce anywhere. He looked forward to continuing the culture change that he had started five years earlier. As it turned out, this would be his last move within GM. He remained plant manager at the Tonawanda Engine Plant for thirteen years until his retirement. What he was able to accomplish in those thirteen years will be the subject of the next several chapters.

POSTSCRIPT

The success of Don's efforts in changing the culture in the Tonawanda Forge Plant was short-lived because General Motors decided to spin it off in 1994 as part of an independent company called the American Axle Company. This new company would supply GM with the forgings it needed for its auto plants. In retrospect, this spinoff was a colossal human disaster for the workforce. The new company entered an industrial war with its unions that led to costly strikes and, ultimately, to the decision by American Axle to move all its U.S. operations to Mexico. This led to massive layoffs of U.S. workers. One can only wonder what would have happened if American Axle had continued the culture change at the Tonawanda Forge Plant, enhancing its productivity. Instead, the leaders of American Axle followed the traditional strategy of treating workers as expendable, a variable expense that could be reduced by exporting production to a country with a lower-cost workforce.

CHAPTER 9

Saving the Tonawanda Engine Plant

I n Chapters 7 and 8, we described Don's early experiences in GM's Tonawanda campus of auto plants. Don took on assignments at both the engine plant and the forge plant, changing the culture within his leadership domain at each. Then, in 1983, the Chevrolet Division of GM asked Don to return to the engine plant, but this time as plant manager. It was a rather sudden and unexpected turn of events and a great opportunity for Don. During his first assignment there, which lasted two years, he had come to appreciate the quality of the management and the people who did the job of bolting a wide variety of GM engines together.

Don was aware that things had not been going very well at the engine plant for the past two years because production had dropped off significantly due to a severe slowing of the nation's economy. As a result, the second shift had been eliminated with a layoff of about 2,500 workers. This, added to the lack of new business, was putting the plant in a precarious position. This was GM's largest engine plant, and it was greatly underutilized. It was also the year that a new national and local labor contract should have been negotiated with the UAW. The national contract had been settled during the year, but the local contract negotiations were stalled; management and the union seemed to be at an impasse, with little progress in coming to an agreement.

A PLANT IN CRISIS

Within the first few days of Don's return to the engine plant, it was apparent that this was not the same engine plant he had left some five years before: he saw that there was now a full-blown industrial depression in progress. This, in addition to the poor demand for engines caused by an economic recession, presented serious threats to the long-term viability of the plant. Labor and management could not agree on a labor contract, which always creates hard feelings among both workers and management. There was very little enthusiasm for the day-to-day activities that normally make work days interesting. It was abundantly clear that Don had inherited a mess. He knew that the first few days in his new job as plant manager would be critical if there were to be any hope of turning things around quickly—or at all.

The first staff meeting after a manager change usually presents a good opportunity to clear the air on what the staff could expect in the way of day-to-day operations. For starters, Don announced that his office door would be open to anyone who needed to talk to him. Don recalled how a similar step with Frank Cantafio had set the foundation for building a successful relationship between management and the second-shift workers back when he had first arrived. Today, his office had been locked for the past five years due to some perceived threats that GM had experienced. One high-level corporate manager's son had been kidnapped during that time. While it didn't seem like a very big announcement, Don's adopting an open-door policy clearly signaled a change in direction that many of the staff and workers liked. Before that first meeting ended, Don announced that he would, within a very few days, call for an urgent meeting of the staff and the union officers to draw up a plan that would attempt to turn the plant in a more positive direction. One can only imagine what must have gone through the minds of Don's management team when he invited the union officers to attend this meeting.

Not long after Don took over the Tonawanda plant, he was summoned to Detroit to Chevrolet headquarters for a one-on-one visit with the president of the Chevrolet Division of GM. At that meeting, Don was told he would not have much time to make some big changes because it was generally accepted in Detroit that the Tonawanda plant was too big to be managed, and consequently there was the likelihood that it could be one of the plants to be closed. Don was also told that the Tonawanda plant would need to get some new business going as soon as possible if a closure were to be avoided. At the same time, the president pointed out that there was little chance for new business until a local labor contract was signed. With all this news, Don was eager to return to the plant and get started on doing what was necessary to change its fate. He resolved to rally both management and the union to find a way to save the Tonawanda Engine Plant. He knew there was no choice, and his career and the careers of thousands of GM workers were at stake.

CREATING A PLAN FOR CHANGE

Don scheduled a big staff meeting immediately upon his return from Detroit. He delivered the clear message that he had received during his meeting with the president of the Chevrolet Division, and he sensed a high level of interest from the staff and the union officers in keeping the plant alive. This was a good sign, and it quickly led to a dialogue to address the challenges facing the plant. In turn, the dialogue led to a plan for the upcoming year. A chart identifying each challenge and goal that was agreed upon was drawn and hung on the wall (see Figure 9-1, following). It was a simple chart, and when the meeting ended, everyone agreed that the goals it depicted were significant and far-reaching. At the same time, both management and the workers expressed optimism that they would be able to achieve their goals—admittedly, with some luck and by working together as a team.

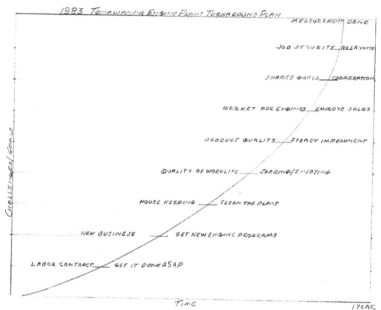

Figure 9-1: Challenges and Goals for the Tonawanda Engine Plant, 1983

As shown on the chart, the first goal was to get back to the negotiating table to carve out a labor agreement that workers could understand and ratify. This was accomplished within two weeks. The second goal was to look for a way to bring in some new business. Don knew that Chevrolet had two new cars coming forward, the Corsica and the Beretta, and each would need a new style of engine. The engines would be a new V-six and a new four-cylinder. The Tonawanda plant had enough available floor space to accommodate production of both engines, but traditionally, most plants could only handle one new engine at a time due to the complexity and intensity of setting the lines up and having them ready for production. Don knew taking on production of two new engines simultaneously was a bold move by him and his management team.

A NEW BEGINNING

With the blessing of the union leadership, the management team decided to submit a bid to Chevrolet for both engines. The team outlined how doing both could save time and money by sharing space and labor. They also showed how the installation costs would be lower when applied at one location. The team members held their collective breath for a couple of weeks while the proposals were studied by Chevrolet top management. When the decision was announced that the Tonawanda Engine Plant would get both engines, it was like winning the Super Bowl. It had not been lost on Don that the signing of a labor agreement within two weeks of his meeting with the president of Chevrolet had been a signal to the top managers that the plant was serious about staying in business—and ready to demonstrate it with concrete action on the agreement. That GM management apparently recognizing this commitment by awarding the plant both new engines was a strong statement of support for the plant.

It would be hard to adequately describe the change in the mood of everyone in the plant, but there was definitely a boost in spirits. But the challenge of getting the two lines up and operating was enormous, and there was little time for celebrating. Everyone knew hard work was ahead of them, and much was at stake to honor the commitment they had made. There were many other goals on the chart that needed to be addressed. Housekeeping had deteriorated during the past two years, and the plant needed to be cleaned up. Another goal was to improve the quality of work life in the plant. One methodology used to accomplish this was by sharing daily updates to the workers of progress on how the plan depicted on the chart was moving forward. Don was fervent about this. He believed that workers needed and deserved to know everything that goes into making a large plant like Tonawanda percolate on a daily basis. He believed that work was a lot more interesting if everyone felt they had a role to play and were contributing to a major cause, like staying in business. His background in farming played a major role in shaping this thinking.

Another important goal that needed attention was the quality of the engines. Don invited everyone to find ways to assemble engines that would improve their quality and, ultimately, customer satisfaction. As a result, there was a tremendous effort to make sure the plant's newest engines would be a huge success.

One of the biggest concerns at the time was whether the two new cars from Chevrolet would sell well enough to keep the plant in business. With that thought in mind, the team decided to actually get involved with the marketing and sales of those cars. The team put a program together that would include all employees at the Tonawanda Engine Plant. The idea was that all employees would identify prospective customers who could be sent to Chevrolet dealers for a sale. This initiative was called "The Chevrolet Sales Team," and it got everyone's interest. Rewards and recognition were offered for anyone who made a referral that led to a confirmed sale. Several young GM workers from Detroit supported this effort and contributed their own ideas to help the program. The Chevrolet Sales Team challenge is discussed in detail in Chapter 16.

BUILDING A NEW ERA OF LABOR COLLABORATION

As the team progressed in tackling its plan and having some success, it became apparent that the union and management employees were even more eager to participate in the shared goals. They wanted to be involved in the planning and decision-making. They wanted to share in the successes that were expected to take place. There was a level of cooperation among all workers that was unprecedented at the Tonawanda plant. It was exciting to watch the interest level continue to rise as the program came into action. It was like playing in the Super Bowl—and winning.

A major goal for workers was job security. That subject was one of the most important items discussed at the planning meeting and added to the chart. Everyone was aware of the pain caused by the long-term layoff of 2,500 workers. Finding a solution to the job security challenge was a high priority.

At the conclusion of the planning session, a timeline had been established to meet all goals. And, while it may have seemed aggressive, there was a commitment to complete all the goals within one year of the planning session. It was an ambitious plan for sure, and none of the participants were convinced they could pull it off.

But one year later, when the final review took place, each and every goal on the chart had been reached. There was a strong sense of pride surrounding this achievement and a newfound momentum that would catapult the workforce into a new way of life at the plant. It was a true culture change. What proved even more surprising was that, as time went on, the culture change became a way of life at the plant. Thirty-two years later, through five changes in the plant manager, the Tonawanda Engine Plant has maintained its strong, upbeat culture. It retains its stature as GM's largest and one of the best engine plants. The remaining chapters will describe, in detail, how the initiatives were implemented that led up to this change of culture.

PART THREE:
UNDERSTANDING CULTURE

CHAPTER 10

Industrial Depression

D on's early experiences at the Tonawanda Engine Plant manufacturing complex were very different from the high level of energy and productivity he had experienced in the Traffic Department or in the Saginaw Engine Plant described in Chapters 5 and 6. In the Tonawanda Engine Plant, the workers were angry, even hostile, toward management. Absenteeism and turnover were high. The workers who did show up had little energy. Don heard comments like, "I would never want any of my family to work at this plant."

IDENTIFYING AND DEFINING INDUSTRIAL DEPRESSION

When Don asked workers why they felt that way, the answers were strikingly similar from one worker to another. They did not look forward to getting up on Monday morning, or any other morning, for that matter, to return to their jobs. In some cases, they did not like the particular job they were asked to perform day after day after day. Some did not like working for their particular supervisor. Others expressed negative feelings about the company in general. Overall, they had negative feelings about management and felt they could not place their trust in their managers. Then there were those who had no faith in the job security offered by the company. They knew they could be laid off any time the company experienced negative financial results, a drop in sales, or any other kind of economic distress. For all these reasons, and perhaps many more, the comfort of being in control of their lives and the economic support of their families was uncertain and contributed to what we have identified as "industrial depression."

Exactly what is industrial depression? What causes it, and how is it manifested in behavior? Table 10-1 lists the most common causes and effects of industrial depression.

CAUSE	EFFECT
Bully management style	Negative attitudes
Feeling expendable	Absenteeism
Dehumanizing stereotypes	High turnover
Fear of layoffs	Job protection
Short-term emphasis on profits	Poor performance

Table 10-1: Causes and Effects of Industrial Depression

Next, we will explain the causes and effects described in Table 10-1

When a worker is bullied, the natural response is to harbor negative feelings toward the perpetrator. There was ample evidence that workers at the Tonawanda Engine Plant were bullied by managers and supervisors.

Workers not only expressed negative attitudes toward management, but they withheld cooperation with management's initiatives. This negative behavior would have a devastating impact on GM's ability to compete against foreign imports in the 1970s and 1980s.

Management's attitude toward workers had been to treat them as expendable. Jobs were routinized to an extent that they were repetitive and boring, controlled by an assembly line that paced work activity. In response, workers took advantage of negotiated liberal work rules that allowed them to call in sick and still maintain their jobs. If a worker brought in a doctor's statement supporting illness, the sick day was not charged against him or her. Workers took advantage of this policy, which spawned a scam with doctors who sympathized with them by writing them a statement just for the asking. Absenteeism was a major problem in staffing, requiring the plant to hire additional workers to fill in for absent workers.

Not every worker would tolerate the negative stereotype of the typical plant worker. Those who were able to find jobs in less hostile environments left. The workers who stayed became hardened to management's treatment, which contributed to the poor morale and ingrained resistance to management's initiatives. Those who stayed also played a game of withholding production, believing that this might somehow protect their job and reduce the likelihood of layoffs. Losing their job was something workers feared greatly. The UAW successfully negotiated work rules to give workers some protection from layoffs, hampering management's ability to make staffing decisions.

General Motors kept a close eye on the financial performance of its divisions. The Tonawanda Engine Plant was no exception. Decisions were often made based upon short-term goals that would enhance the monthly financial statements of the corporation. Budgets were closely watched for any spending overages. No one in the plant knew how much its engine production output contributed to profits. They only knew how well they performed to budget. This led to behaviors that directly affected quality and performance. Frequently, the emphasis was to make quotas and ship products out the door, even when quality was poor.

We define industrial depression as a feeling of despair and a sense of being devalued, and it is often demonstrated by a lack of energy among workers suffering from it. It can't be seen except by its symptoms or consequences. However, we believe it is very real and very costly.

It is hard to understand why industrial depression has not been recognized. Industrial psychologists and other students of organizations have studied extensively the negative effects of meaningless jobs, toxic leadership, and negative cultures, but they have not identified a syndrome that saps workers of their value and energy.

CONSEQUENCES OF INDUSTRIAL DEPRESSION

Industrial depression can affect one worker, a group of workers, or, in the more extreme cases, an entire workforce. It can envelop workers like a fog that prevents them from seeing where they are going. Workers suffering from industrial depression will keep going to work but only because they need their wages to support themselves and their family. They will only put forth enough effort to keep their job. They will not worry about the effect their lack of effort has on the company's performance. In fact, many workers believe that holding back their effort and slowing down the pace of work will add to their job security.

Now, imagine the consequences of an organization's entire workforce experiencing industrial depression. This has the makings of a financial disaster, and this is exactly what happened to General Motors.

A closer look at the industrially depressed worker leads us to the subject of human energy, because it is the worker's human energy that must be released to perform the job at hand. Industrially depressed workers withhold this human energy. Expending energy is a decision that only the worker can make. Douglas McGregor, in his classic book *The Human Side of Enterprise*, discusses the conditions under which human energy is either released or withheld. According to McGregor, the condition under which energy is withheld by the worker is called "Theory X." Under Theory X conditions, managers believe their workers are inherently lazy and negative toward work. Theory X conditions lead to micromanaging, strong disciplinary programs, and aggressive tactics by managers to get work done. "Theory Y," on the other hand, is the belief that workers are inherently creative and eager to work. This belief will encourage managers to value workers and treat them fairly, which, in turn, will lead to workers being willing to expend effort and perform at a high level.

Human energy has been studied from many angles over the years, but to date no one has been able to measure it. Management has always considered it their prerogative to demand more work (that is, that workers must release more of their energy than they are willing to release toward their job), but it is common knowledge that there is no better way to turn off workers' enthusiasm than by demanding more work from them. If, in fact, a worker had a positive relationship with management, that relationship would deteriorate rapidly when confronted with a bona fide demand to release more energy than the worker is comfortable with.

If anyone were to reflect on the earlier years in the development of the automobile manufacturing business, he or she would find many of the precursors of industrial depression. Management had a reputation for abusive behavior toward its workers in those years. Workers were undoubtedly exposed to many, if not all, of the conditions that lead to industrial depression. In those days, however, workers found a way to neutralize the heavy hand of management and organized a union, the UAW. Not only did they organize, but they went on the infamous sit-down strike at the Flint GM plant in 1936. It could be said that the workers fought back in those early days, attempting to neutralize the power that management exercised over their work lives. This strategy surely required a great deal of energy. Unfortunately, instead of reforming its management approach, GM management dug its heels in deeper, creating a strong negative attitude toward the union. And, while the union may have neutralized the arbitrary power of management, the antagonism and dysfunction bred by this warfare between union and management led to the conditions that spawned industrial depression.

INDUSTRIAL DEPRESSION: A COMPARISON OF TWO INDUSTRIES

It is interesting to look at whether industrial depression was just prevalent in the auto industry or whether it was widespread across other industries. There have been widespread reports of serious labor/management feuds in other industries, including meat packing, service industries, earth-moving equipment manufacturers, coal mining, and aircraft builders, to name just a few. We believe industrial depression is widespread throughout most industries, and especially prevalent in those with poor labor relations. The level of damage caused to productivity by sapping energy from the workforce is a major factor in making our industries less competitive. In this chapter, we will limit our discussion to the agriculture and auto-manufacturing industries, but by no means does this imply that these are the only industries suffering from industrial depression.

Farmers are the producers of our food. They are, for the most part, both independent business people and the workers who are employed to work on their farms. We do not make a distinction between farm owners and farm workers. Farmers and their workers have complete control over the energy they expend toward their everyday work life. They are totally responsible for the decisions they make in the course of every day while managing their farms. They also have to deal with tremendous obstacles, such as the weather, the economy, crop disease and pests, and human fatigue. It is rare that farmers or farmhands leave their jobs each day at 5 p.m. and go home to their families. They generally work until dark or until the job is done for that day. They then get up at the crack of dawn to begin a new day of challenges in order to grow the food that feeds our nation.

When comparing people who work on farms with factory workers, one can readily draw some major conclusions. Unlike factory workers, farmers and farmhands are basically happy people. They like the work they do. They pay little attention to the length of their typical workday. The day is done when the work is done. A great deal of their satisfaction comes from the quality of their efforts, specifically in terms of improving their productivity and the quality of their products. They don't rely on managers to tell them what to do. And, in spite of the obstacles they face from weather, the markets, pests, and their own fatigue, farm workers continue to expend the energy needed to be successful.

There is camaraderie among farmers in general. They tend to look out for each other. They often work closely together on a given task, especially at times when another farmer is struck with illness or an accident. Neighboring farmers will never leave the stricken farmer's fields untended or allow the stricken farmer's harvest to die in the fields. They are well aware that they, too, operate at the mercy of whatever Mother Nature or fate can throw at them, and they, too, could be in a similar situation when an illness or accident strikes. Farmers accept the risk of making major investments required to plant their fields, raise their livestock, and bring it all to a conclusion at each harvest time. They know that their workers will step up to the challenges demanded of them.

While farmers and their farmhands certainly have plenty to contend with, they don't have to put up with the boring and monotonous jobs given to workers in manufacturing plants. They don't have to put up with an operating contract that attempts to micromanage and specify every facet of what they do all day. If farmers are successful, their success is entirely theirs to enjoy. We are unaware of any farmer or farm worker who has ever restricted the release of his or her energy due to industrial depression.

In light of the foregoing comparison of two distinctly different industries, it becomes easier to understand why factory workers might easily become depressed with their jobs while farmers and farm workers enjoy a significantly different and better quality of work life. It therefore seems fair to ask what any of us can learn from farming that can help the auto industry change its culture and eliminate the industrial depression that is sapping its energy and vitality.

What would it take to change the culture so significantly in the factory that the workers would get excited about the employer they work for and involve themselves in their work to the greatest extent possible? What would it take to change the manufacturing culture so workers would look forward to going to work every day? What would it take to change the culture so workers would harbor the same goals as the managers and the company they work for? What would it take to change the culture, so workers could enjoy real job security? What would it mean to the workers if they could actually be involved in the major decisions regarding the operation of the company they work for?

This discussion is rather long, but it is important and necessary if one is to look seriously at changing the culture of factories and eliminating industrial depression. Perhaps more importantly, all of us need to start to understand why a manufacturing culture plagued by industrial depression needs to change. The answers may lie in borrowing from the values exhibited in other industries, such as agriculture.

CHAPTER 11

A Practical Discussion of Human Energy

The subject of physical energy has been extensively studied. Whether it is Einstein's Theory of Relativity or electricity flowing through a wire, everyone understands that energy is released when certain physical conditions are met. This scientific approach to physical energy is an excellent metaphor for understanding human energy. It helps us to be aware of the sources of energy and the conditions that allow energy to flow. It also makes us aware of conditions that lead to energy resistance, or interruptions in the flow of energy.

In studying how workers treat their jobs, we have chosen to study human energy rather than the traditional concept of motivation. We believe motivation is an important concept, but energy, ultimately, is what propels activity. While motivation must be inferred deep in the human psyche, energy and its results can be viewed more directly in human activity. The more activity, the more energy is expended. How to stimulate humans to release energy is a challenge as old as the human workplace, and it is a question that lies at the heart of any endeavor requiring human energy for success.

Just what are the optimal conditions for the expenditure of human energy? We would argue that these conditions are dependent on the individual, the culture, and the source of the energy request. In a work situation, the individual would be the worker, the culture would be the environmental conditions of the workplace, and the source of the energy request is the demands made on the worker, usually coming from some level of supervision or management.

In a situation demanding a high level of production, with a positive culture in place, and workers willing to do what it takes to meet work demands, the level of energy will be high. In contrast, when the work is demanding and the culture is hostile toward the worker, workers will likely show resistance to any attempt to have pressure exerted on them to increase their level of energy expended. In this scenario, energy is likely to be low, and a low level of output will be the result. We will use this framework to analyze human energy in General Motors. We believe that human energy is what turns the wheels of production and work output. Under the right conditions, human energy will flow freely and yield high output. The challenge is for management to create the conditions that will yield a high level of energy and output.

Behavioral scientists have created several concepts to describe positive conditions. The concept we choose to use is culture. Culture is defined by the norms of the organization and its traditions, values, and shared beliefs. When the culture is positive and constructive, energy should flow with little resistance. Conversely, when the culture is negative and destructive, the demands of work will likely be met with resistance, inhibiting energy and lowering work output.

THE INDIVIDUAL

People vary greatly in their level of energy. All of us know individuals who have a great deal of energy. Unlike measuring physical energy, there is not a good yardstick for measurement of human energy. Each of us infers individual levels of human energy from activities. The more active people are, the more energy is attributed to them. It should be noted that energy may not always be expended toward positive organizational goals. But we can positively say that energy and activity are highly correlated.

One of the earliest studies of human energy was performed by Frederick Taylor at the Bethlehem Steel Company. Taylor, considered the father of industrial engineering, observed steel workers and how they physically performed their jobs. Based upon the activity of the worker, he would retrain them in how to better use motion and energy to perform the tasks of their job. Taylor was able to increase work output with his methodology by helping workers to make more money if they cooperated with the changes he proposed. Unlike how Taylor's original studies of the efficient use of energy were used in the steel industry, the auto industry used his methodologies to establish standard times for each operation. This allowed for unit pricing in GM's financial system.

From the worker's perspective, industrial engineers ran their studies simply to speed up work. In the auto plant, it was common practice to send industrial engineers into operating areas with a clipboard and a stopwatch. They would stand near a worker performing a particular job and time every element of the work associated with a given task. At the completion of the time study, a decision would be made as to whether the worker was contributing the right amount of energy to the task. If it appeared to be too low, the worker would be told to put more effort (that is, energy) into the task in order to increase production.

Overall, these time and motion studies may have contributed to some improvement in productivity, but not without cost. In the auto industry, time and motion studies were one of the most antagonistic activities in the workplace, and they quite often ended up generating a grievance procedure from the worker's union representative. If there appeared to be a real attempt to increase the level of effort workers were expected to exert, the union had the option of filing a speed-up grievance, and if not resolved, it could lead to a strike. Clearly, the pressure to influence workers to increase their effort or productivity was met with resistance because elements in their culture resisted the demands for increased energy.

THE CULTURE

The culture in the auto industry for the past eight decades has been hostile. In the earliest days of the auto industry, the culture could be considered paternalistic. Thankful to have decent-paying jobs during trying economic times, workers complied with the demands of work. After the Flint sit-down strike of 1936, things changed. Management viewed workers and their union as enemies. In return, workers, through their union, created protections against any change that management proposed that would lead to increased energy to perform their jobs. Every GM plant had a local union, and a great deal of energy was used to fight an undeclared war between the union and management. The symptoms of this conflict were work slowdowns, spontaneous "wildcat" strikes, filing of grievances, high worker absenteeism and turnover, and a lack of any cooperation that would energize the workforce. This is one reason why management and industrial engineering failed to deliver on their promise. While its principles were sound, the resistance in the culture rendered any attempts to apply these principles futile.

Over the years, the hostility between the union and management increased. A set of norms were created within management that viewed workers and their union as the enemy. Management also viewed workers as disposable. Any sign of a business slowdown would lead to layoffs, putting workers out of work until business turned around.

This was the predominant culture of the auto manufacturing industry through the first fifty or so years of its existence.

In 1983, when Don took over the Tonawanda Engine Plant, the least-senior worker had fourteen years of experience. Twenty-five-hundred workers with less than fourteen years' seniority had been laid off. It was clear to workers and the union that GM used the workforce as a variable expense to adjust to business cycles. It was also clear that the hostile environment prevented any cooperation between workers and management to solve the problems of work output, product quality, restrictive work rules, escalating salaries and benefits, absenteeism, turnover, monotonous work, and job security, just to name the most obvious issues. Whatever energy existed was misdirected into norms that kept management and union at war.

THE SOURCE

In the 1960s, GM was the leader in U.S. automobile sales, with 60 percent of the domestic market. The company was able to compete with other domestic auto manufacturers through excellent marketing and distribution. It could afford to pay higher wages and benefits than its competitors and still make healthy profits for shareholders. From the outside, GM was a very successful company. Even with a hostile culture, the company was blessed by the American love for automobiles, cheap fuel, and a road system that enabled easy travel throughout the country. GM prospered. This all changed in 1974, when the first oil embargo dramatically curtailed the supply of gasoline. Gasoline was rationed and its price soared. American automobiles were gas guzzlers compared to foreign automobiles that were quickly entering the U.S. market.

Consumers acted in their best interest and began to buy smaller, more fuel-efficient autos.

This was a major turning point in the domestic auto industry, and GM was the hardest hit by the changes in demand from the American consumer. Instead of making peace with the union, the culture became even more hostile at GM. Under severe economic pressure, GM began sourcing parts out of the country, angering workers and their union. The attempts to speed up production led to even more labor strife through grievances and work slowdowns. It was no surprise that one of the tactics used by workers was to expend less energy and slow production in order to preserve their jobs. To workers, expending more energy, as demanded by management, would only lead to more layoffs and loss of wages. Management failed to explain to workers that more output generally meant more margin and profit and greater investment in people and equipment. On the latter point, it is not clear that workers would have believed management, given the level of mistrust that existed between the two groups.

The oil embargo and demand for fuel-efficient autos caught GM by surprise. The company was not able to harness the energy of the workforce to meet the new market demands for fuel-efficient autos. And, as foreign automobile manufacturers improved their quality and productivity through cooperation with their workers and unions, and the use of statistical process control, U.S. auto manufacturers were at a disadvantage. GM quickly lost market share to Toyota, Honda, Datsun, Volkswagen, Volvo, and many other imported brands. The once dominant U.S. auto manufacturer was just not able to overcome the damage it had created in its workforce. The once powerful source of energy had lost its power. It was unable to overcome the resistance it had created.

The norms of the worker enforced human-energy conservation, not energy utilization. This was fueled by a failed management style that tried to force workers into expending more energy. It was this kind of management that pushed workers into industrial depression. Workers would find themselves going to work every day but only contributing the minimum amount of energy to their jobs. Workers paid a high price for this norm and its consequences, both in job security and in psychological health.

Given these circumstances, it was not surprising that high levels of productivity were almost unheard of in GM plants. These plants deteriorated into a kind of war zone between management and labor. The evidence of this battle could be seen in the way management treated workers, and nowhere was it more evident than in the way the first level of management supervision used contractual discipline at every opportunity to keep workers in line. Ironically, the supervisors who issued the most penalties to the workers were often selected for promotion.

The union representatives were not without fault either. They were typically elected to their jobs because they were considered the toughest workers in the plant. They were noted for making sure that no worker made more product than the job called for. They did not encourage the workers to contribute any extra initiative on their job. In fact, they often did the opposite.

The purpose of this discussion about human energy is to demonstrate how the culture at GM carries a great deal of responsibility for the company's failure as a competitive automobile manufacturer. If GM had taken a more positive approach toward labor in its manufacturing plants during those earlier years, the outcome may have been very different. Following the sit-down strike of 1936, GM could have taken the initiative to make peace with workers and their newly formed union. But history tells a different story, one of distrust and animosity between management and labor. In the 1930s, neither party was in any kind of conciliatory mood. What a shame that now, almost eighty years later, there is still not much recognizable effort for management and labor to work in partnership.

In later chapters, we will discuss successful efforts to change the culture at the Tonawanda Engine Plant. A great deal was learned about human energy as a result of this culture change. In a positive culture, unionized workers were energized, and their energy was released toward greater effort and productivity. This energy was not released because of the demands of any controlling level of management. To the contrary, workers participated fully as partners in making changes that were necessary for the Tonawanda plant to be competitive. Early in the 1980s, "Partners in Progress" became the phrase that captured a newly emerging culture at the Tonawanda Engine Plant. We can only speculate about the human energy that could have been generated if management and the newly formed UAW union in the 1930s would have invoked this motto and become "partners in progress" some forty years earlier.

What led to this release of positive energy in the 1980s? We believe when a worker enjoys a good quality of work life, has a positive relationship with management, has a positive feeling about job security, shares in the success of the products produced, and is treated with trust and respect at work, a reservoir of unused energy can be called upon by that worker to do whatever it takes to be successful. Increasing energy expended has always been, and always will be, a strictly voluntary reaction by the worker.

To illustrate this point, on one particular day at the Tonawanda Engine Plant, everyone in that plant contributed their energies to set a world record for engines produced. At no time did anyone in management demand that a new record be set. This was a joint venture. Both management and workers were excited about their quest for a new world record. It was also clear that the same level of energy would not be expected on a daily basis going forward. There could be no clearer evidence that when called upon, human energy is available. The key is to create the culture that allows and encourages it to be released.

In the following chapters, we will describe the preconditions that led to the release of human energy and the elimination of industrial depression at the Tonawanda Engine Plant.

CHAPTER 12

The Caprice Fiasco

In the mid-1980s, GM moved the Chevrolet Caprice assembly operations from Detroit to the Lakewood Assembly Plant near Atlanta, Georgia. It was during the start-up operations at Lakewood that Don had ordered a new Caprice for himself. This was part of an established GM executive purchase program in which the car would be test-driven as a company car for three thousand miles and then could be purchased as a personal vehicle by the executive. The test period was an opportunity to check the vehicle for defects, which would be reported back to the assembly plant as part of its quality control program.

On the day that Don's new Caprice arrived, he happened to look out of his office window and saw an auto transport truck arriving at the plant, not with one but with two new Caprices to be unloaded. One was black, which would have been the one Don had ordered. The prospect of getting a new car had always been an exciting event for Don. With much anticipation, he walked down to where the unloading was taking place in order to look the car over, as required by the test procedures, for any quality problems.

Don's first observation surprised him. There was a large baseball-sized dent in the car's roof, just above the driver's door. It appeared to have been there before the car was painted. He could not imagine that car having been approved for shipment and sale in that condition. A closer inspection revealed numerous other defects, and the fit and finish was a disaster. But worst of all for Don was the front bumper: it was installed off center by six inches. The left end of the bumper was touching the inside edge of the left front fender, while the right end of the bumper was sticking out past the right front fender by six inches. No customer would ever buy a car that exhibited so many quality problems. At that point, Don's righteous indignation kicked in, and he ordered the truck driver to reload the cars for return to the Lakewood Plant. The second car was equally as bad as the one he had ordered.

Perplexed at this unprecedented experience, Don wondered what he should do next. He remembered that at a very recent managers' meeting in Detroit, the vice president of Chevrolet had directed all senior managers, in a manner that could not have been misunderstood, to be very diligent in reporting any quality problems that were observed coming out of their operations. Don decided to first go out to the local Chevrolet dealers and inspect any new Caprice cars in their inventory. This proved to be an even greater disappointment because some of those cars were in worse shape than the two that had been delivered to the plant. Some cars even exhibited incomplete body sheet metal panels, defects that were highly visible.

On return to the plant later that day, Don knew there were cars in the GM system that were not salable. He knew he needed to initiate a course of action that would stop the assembly process at the Lakewood

Plant. He decided to call the plant manager of the Lakewood Plant to tell him about the quality problems he was seeing and suggest that he should consider stopping production immediately. The manager's response was that the Lakewood Plant was in a start-up mode, and the cars would improve over time. Don responded that the cars he saw were not salable and suggested that the plant manager take appropriate action as soon as possible. Refusing to accept Don's suggestion left Don with little choice but to inform the manager that Don would report the problem to officials at Chevrolet headquarters in Detroit. The manager responded with, "Do whatever you want to do about it." This lack of concern or willingness to take action on this obvious disaster left Don in a quandary.

Don's immediate superior was on vacation and could not be reached, so he called the Lakewood plant manager's superior, only to be told by his secretary that he was out of town on business and could not be "bothered." Frustrated, Don decided to call the Chevrolet vice president. He finally had a receptive audience. The VP listened to Don's description of the problems, including his assessment that the cars were not salable. The VP thanked Don for bringing the problem to his attention and stated that he would take ownership of the problem from there. Later, Don found out that the Lakewood plant manager's superior had actually been in that plant, where he couldn't be "bothered." He was apparently the executive who made the decision not to stop production at that time.

The word got out that Don had been the manager who first reported the Caprice problem to Detroit, and many of his fellow manager "friends" openly chastised him for doing it. While shaken by this criticism, Don knew he had done the right thing. He has never regretted taking that course of action at that time.

A short time after Don had alerted Detroit about the Caprice quality issues, the topic, which came to be known as the "Caprice Fiasco," was the subject at a GM general managers' meeting in Detroit. It was announced there that the problem had been corrected. From that point forward, there were never any complaints about the quality of Caprice cars, suggesting that, indeed, Detroit stepped in to make whatever changes were necessary to avoid a major quality issue.

Perhaps better than any other single event within GM at the time, the Caprice Fiasco not only clearly illustrated the magnitude of industrial depression that had settled over Chevrolet and GM but demonstrated its tangible effects. More recently, another major GM quality problem, this one related to faulty ignition switches, has been exposed on a much larger scale, and it demonstrated the same pattern of reluctance toward action that existed decades earlier with the Caprice Fiasco. The only major difference with the ignition switch case is that no one from within GM had stepped forward in time to correct the problem before people lost their lives and it cost GM billions of dollars to correct.

The reader is probably asking, "How could a company like GM allow such an obvious quality problem to go so far before it was remedied?" The answer can be found in the Caprice Fiasco experience. Unless someone is willing to "blow the whistle" and get the attention of executives who can step in and make a change, quality problems are likely to exist. One would like to think this is not a game by top management to avoid responsibility by waiting out angry consumers in the hope that the cost of financial settlements will be less than the cost of disrupting sales. Clearly, this would be a horrible indictment against the company. A more likely reason is the strong norm that exists within management not to report anything negative to upper management—with a clear understanding that if you did, you would be ostracized by your peers. This norm remains strong in spite of the verbal statements by upper management to always report such problems. Sadly, not much has changed in thirty years.

It is interesting to speculate whether industrial depression had a role to play in other recent corporate fiascos, such as the defective Takata air bags, the Volkswagen false diesel-emissions reporting, and the Samsung smartphone's exploding batteries. We believe these problems should have been identified and resolved before the products were introduced to the public. Failure to identify and correct such problems is consistent with cultures that inhibit open and candid dialogue because of fear and norms that promote the wrong goals.

CHAPTER 13

Defining Cultural Change

A search for the definition of "organizational culture" reveals that just about everyone has a different idea about what it is. We chose a simple definition: organizational culture is the way an entity such as a corporation or business is managed. While academics talk about stories, myths, and rituals as ways of describing a culture, we focused our attention on several major areas that have a significant impact on the organization's ability to carry out its mission.

DESCRIBING GM'S CULTURE

We would like to break down culture into three major areas: 1) management's approach to workers, sometimes called "management style"; 2) the nature of work, including working conditions; and 3) the goals of the organization, or what it is trying to accomplish. These three areas incorporate the values and attitudes that exist within the organization.

We have described in some detail the management style that permeated GM production facilities. This style fits very well with human management and motivation theorist Douglas McGregor's Theory X assumptions that workers are lazy, lack initiative, and will do the minimum work required of their jobs. These assumptions led GM management to treat workers with strong controls and negative attitudes, often leading to harsh rules to govern worker behavior. An example of these rules is the detailed discipline manuals created to keep employees in line and to punish them for rule violations. In response to management demands and discipline, workers used their union to protect them, firing back with grievances and, in some cases, strikes to get them what they wanted.

It may sound harsh, but we view the GM management-worker culture as toxic and at times combative.

The second area of culture is the nature of work and working conditions. The auto industry, from the time of Henry Ford, chose the assembly line as its major technological innovation to produce automobiles. GM was no exception. From a cultural perspective, this meant the speed of work was controlled by a conveyer system, with workers performing quick, simple, and repetitive activities. It is not hard to imagine how boring and tedious these jobs were and how they could dampen the human spirit toward work. The bargain that workers and their unions made was to extract high wages and benefits to compensate them for these tedious, boring jobs. The nature of assembly line work only exacerbated the negative attitudes management and workers had toward each other.

The third area of culture relates to the goals of management. In its heyday, GM had a strong reputation as a publicly minded company that produced good products and returned a good dividend to its shareholders. GM executives, rewarding themselves with stock options, prided themselves in earning strong profits for shareholders. To the workers in the production facilities, this meant the goal of meeting bottom-line results was dictated by corporate management. Without the cooperation of the workforce, bottom-line results became more and more difficult to accomplish. Plants began to take shortcuts, allowing poor quality products to be shipped in order to meet delivery demands. This was multiplied through the interdependent system that GM had developed of supplying one plant with parts produced by another. Workers, recognizing the quality problems, were helpless to do anything about it—except lose even more respect for management.

The Caprice Fiasco discussed in the previous chapter is an excellent example of how the need to generate profits destroyed product quality and pride of both GM's corporate managers and workers at the plant level.

INITIATING CULTURE CHANGE

Almost anyone who is granted the opportunity to be a leader will recognize early on that they are expected, and surely want, to create some kind of success. Why else would potential leaders take on the added responsibility and expectation of effort without the promise of the chance to leave a positive impact?

If you have determined that your organization's performance has leveled off or stalled at a point at or below where you think it should be, then a culture change can be and often is the best way to move organizational performance in a positive direction. Understanding the existing culture and its limitations is a first step in making a change. Change will not happen by proclamation. Serious consideration needs to be given to whether those leading the change have the support and commitment of those who will initiate, manage, and embrace the change. Change is a step that is not to be taken lightly.

Change can lead to uncertainty and even discomfort. Leadership must be willing to address these concerns and work through the doubts of those who are reluctant or not willing to change. This may mean personnel will be leaving the organization or that members of the organization will be exploring new ways to relate to each other.

Once the decision to move toward a culture change is made, how does it get started? What will members of the organization hear and see that will give them the impression that change is in the air? How will they react?

These are questions that Don needed to address as he contemplated making a major cultural change at the Tonawanda Engine Plant in 1983. He knew that the workforce would be very sensitive to any changes that impacted its quality of work life. Armed with his strong desire to create a positive work culture and his unyielding commitment to treat workers with faith, trust, and respect, Don embarked on the biggest challenge of his career. He knew this would require a change in management style, and he knew he was taking a path down a one-way street. Don knew that once you go down this path, your particular management style will be visible and measured on a day-to-day basis. Being consistent with the way you meet and treat the workers is mandatory and unconditional. Any inconsistency will slow your efforts and detract from whatever success has been generated to date. It is important to remember that the workers in the auto industry have been exposed to all kinds of inattention and, in some cases, a level of abuse that has caused them to be suspicious of almost any change coming from management. This can impede any culture change effort that confronts them.

If you ask Don about how to initiate and sustain culture change, here is what he would tell you:

Workers are normally very perceptive when change seems to be in the air. If you want them to know that you trust them, look for ways to get that message out, and keep that trust on display at all times. Hot and cold just doesn't work in moving a culture change forward. If you want them to know that you have respect for them as workers and as individuals, you have to demonstrate your respect for them in as many ways as possible. If you want them to know that you have faith in them as workers, then let it show so they can see it. Now cultivate it. (That is my old farmer background coming out again.) A farmer prepares the soil first, and then he plants the seeds. When the seeds germinate, you can see the results as small plants start to come through the surface. The farmer then cultivates the soil to control the weeds and keep the soil soft. At some point, he may even add some fertilizer to sustain and accelerate the growth of the plants. Eventually, the plants mature and the harvest begins. Perhaps a background on the farm isn't the worst thing you can take with you to the big plant. And so it is with creating and sustaining a culture change.

One of the most satisfying events in creating a culture change is when workers reciprocate the faith, trust, and respect shown them by their management. It may happen very slowly, but that is to be expected. Plant workers are naturally suspicious, and, while hopeful, they don't want to overreact to what appears to be a change in management's style. It is important to reach out to the workers, to spend as much time as possible on the plant floor, being available to answer questions they may have, and to listen to their ideas about ways to improve their jobs. Most workers appreciate knowing they can approach their management at any level on a daily basis, or as often as is necessary. This complements their daily quality of work life.

DRIVERS OF CULTURE CHANGE AT GM

In our discussion of initiating culture change, we have focused mostly on leadership and a change in management style. In future chapters, we will describe what we call "drivers of culture change" at GM. These are the areas that needed attention but were embedded in a toxic culture that ignored them and that we believe ultimately drove GM to threaten the closure of the Tonawanda Engine Plant. We will identify each of these cultural drivers and share how each was changed. The results were a remarkable turnaround from a plant that almost closed to what is today one of the most successful engine manufacturing plants in the world.

What are these drivers of culture change? Table 13-1 lists the drivers that Don and his management team focused on and the contribution of each toward culture change at GM. In the table, we have identified the original culture and the culture change that took place.

OLD GM CULTURE	NEW GM CULTURE
Layoff Mentality	Job Security
Boring, Repetitive Work	Making Work Interesting
Isolating Workers from the Business	Involving Workers in the Business
Poor Quality	A Passion for Excellence
Bully Management	Caring Management
All Work and No Play	Celebrations
Singular Focus on Profits	Doing the Right Thing for All Stakeholders

Table 13-1: Drivers of GM Culture Change

In Chapters 14 through 21, we will describe in detail just how these drivers of culture were implemented and the outcomes that resulted from the shift in culture they brought about.

PART FOUR:
CHANGING THE EXISTING
CULTURE

CHAPTER 14

The Layoff Problem

From its early years as an industry, auto manufacturing faced a dilemma. Its product sales were cyclical. When the economy was strong, autos sold well. When there was a downturn in the economy, sales dried up. This left the automobile manufacturers with a challenge: what do they do with workers when their product sales are weak? The strategy that emerged was to lay off workers when auto sales were poor and hire them back when sales returned. This has been the strategy for the entire history of the auto industry.

In the boom years of the auto industry, workers were in many cases brought in from the southern states, where well-paying jobs were scarce. Immigrants, mostly from Eastern Europe, also sought employment in the auto industry. These workers were poorly educated and dependent on their companies for a steady income to support themselves and their families. The industry strategy was to protect its major shareholders, and company executives treated workers as a variable expense. This allowed them to shrink or expand the workforce in step with sales. There were no provisions in place that would sustain the workers' incomes during times of layoff, and they often found themselves in desperate situations, with little or no money to support their families until they would get recalled to work. There wasn't even certainty that they would be hired back when sales picked up.

From the workers' perspective, this was a tragic set of circumstances. Their poor education left them with few alternatives for employment. What little opportunity they had to improve their economic status during prosperous industry years was lost during periods of layoff, when they had no income. Many of the homes and autos they purchased when employed were sacrificed when they could no longer afford them after a layoff.

The willingness of workers to tolerate layoffs and poor treatment in general changed in 1936, when workers engaged in the sit-down strike at the Chevrolet Engine Plant in Flint, Michigan. It was the workers' hope that they could get a settlement with GM regarding layoffs that might bring forth some help from a newly formed United Auto Workers union. It was not to be. The UAW succeeded in becoming a part of the ever-expanding auto industry, and it would be there representing the workers—but without a solution to the layoff problem.

GM's layoff strategy became institutionalized over the years. There was some recognition of the layoff problem, but no real solutions came from the new international and local labor contracts that were being negotiated and adopted. Over time, the government stepped in with programs that would give the laid-off workers some limited financial relief to tide them over until they were called back to work, but it was insufficient to really fill in for their lost wages. The UAW also negotiated supplemental unemployment benefits (SUB) for laid-off workers. However, nothing could really take the place of actually having a steady job and paycheck every week.

With the passing of nearly a century of job layoffs, management and the unions to date have not solved this problem. Management's position has been that they couldn't pay people who were not working because it was simply too costly to do so. It was more than clear to even the casual observer that the bottom line was more important than the worker's job security. The unions made numerous attempts to propose changes in their workers' contracts that would alleviate the problem, but in the long run they, too, were unsuccessful. Workers came to expect layoffs as a part of their employment. As mentioned earlier, the UAW was able to negotiate SUB to help workers with short-term layoffs, but the loss of self-esteem from losing their jobs for longer periods of time has been devastating to workers, and there wasn't much they could do about it. One can only wonder what it was like for workers to live with the insecurity of not knowing when the day would come that they would again be told they were not needed for an indefinite period of time or, worse, maybe forever. It had to be devastating for workers to tell their families that the paychecks would not be coming to pay for groceries, medical care, mortgages, car payments, and education for their children.

In Chapter 9, we described the situation Don Rust inherited when he was named plant manager of the Tonawanda Engine Plant. The plant had been through more than five years of economic woes. Production schedules were cut back severely, with only one shift operating. Over 2,500 workers had been laid off. On the day that Don's appointment was announced, it was unknown what the future of the plant would be. There were rumors coming from Detroit that the plant was too big to manage and was listed as one that could possibly be closed in the future.

Don was in a difficult spot. How was he going to manage a plant with so many problems and with rumors swirling that it might be closed? And, how was he going to deal with the fears and insecurities of workers who had lost faith in management and its ability to lead a successful business?

But far and away his biggest challenge was how to get the workforce, which had been decimated by layoffs, to believe in him and his team enough to turn the plant around.

THE CALLBACK

In 1984, with GM's agreement to give the Tonawanda Engine Plant its two new engines to manufacture, it was time to start calling the 2,500 workers on long-term layoff back to their jobs in the plant. Knowing it would be a significant, emotional event for the workers to finally return to their jobs, Don planned to make it as eventful as possible for them. They returned in groups of thirty or more at a time, which allowed for an orderly assimilation back to life in the plant. On the first day of their return, they were invited by Don to a breakfast or lunch and a briefing to update them about the activities currently going on in the plant. Don emphasized the important role they would play in getting the new engines manufactured as well as working on the engines already being produced. During this meeting, Don and his management team deliberately took the time to welcome the workers back. They were not going to rush them to their jobs before making them feel they were once again part of the workforce and with an important role to play in the plant's success.

Don reflected on his feelings about these first meetings with workers. He recalled how heartbreaking it was to listen to their stories of how they survived over the five years of their layoff. Many of them found minimal jobs that paid little but gave them some semblance of hope for a better day ahead. In the meantime, many ran through their life savings they had put away before the layoff, and they had to make difficult family decisions such as giving up their car and house due to their inability to pay loans. They told stories of conversations they had with their college-age children, telling them there would be no money for college. Many workers shared that they experienced depression, which added complications to leading the family through tough times. In some cases, the families broke up, and it wasn't hard to spot the tears as those stories were told. This is what happens to workers and their families when they are laid off for a long period of time. The human tragedy of layoffs had taken its toll. Being able to talk about their experiences was therapeutic, allowing workers to vent their feelings before returning to their jobs.

In 1984, the plant was back to full-time production, although with fewer workers. The recession had ended, and things were beginning to look more like prosperity again. But everyone wanted to know how long this prosperity would last. Having experienced a five-year layoff, was it any wonder that a worker might have second thoughts about overproducing on the job? It was not unusual to hear that union officials would caution workers about exceeding whatever was considered normal output on their jobs. The psychological reality was not to overexert yourself to gain more production output when it would just hasten the day to your next layoff. However, Don knew that this kind of thinking would dampen the recovery and mark a step back into the old ways, and he knew he needed to do something to prevent it.

ELIMINATING LAYOFFS

Anticipating the reluctance of returning workers to invest their energy into making the Tonawanda Engine Plant a success, Don took a bold step. He made the decision to promise workers there would be no more layoffs under his watch. He communicated this promise to each worker on the first day back from layoff, proclaiming that as long as he was their plant manager, there would be no more layoffs unless there was a complete downturn in the auto industry and the economy. In that case, Don proclaimed, everyone would lose their jobs. For obvious reasons, Don did not report to GM that he had just implemented a no-layoff promise to his workers. He knew that GM would not give him the approval for something that drastic. He also knew that setting a no-layoff precedent at the Tonawanda Engine Plant would likely ensure an early end to his career. Don knew that layoffs were a major obstacle to mutual trust and respect. He took a risk that he believed would improve plant performance and more than offset any costs generated by keeping the workforce intact.

When asked about the impact of his no-layoff policy, Don stated that it was nothing short of fascinating to watch what happened to productivity and the sense of pride that workers expressed. There was no question that productivity increased in the months and years after his no-layoff policy was put in force. Don had been aware of how important job security was, and still is, for workers in the auto industry: it was their number one priority. It baffled him to try to understand why the industry ignored solving this problem for so long. In his mind, there seemed to be too many auto executives more interested in short-term profits rather than finding a solution to the most divisive issue that separated management and workers. GM, in particular, had missed a great opportunity to improve its relationship with workers and count on them to be part of a highly effective team.

The Tonawanda Engine Plant went thirteen years under Don's leadership without a single permanent layoff, and this occurred even though there were many times when it appeared a layoff could not be avoided. A true partnership seemed to emerge among Don, his management team, workers, and union officials. It was like some mysterious force had taken over, as evidenced by worker enthusiasm and effort. One of the subjects Don always covered in his quarterly meetings was "how long it had been since the last layoff." The workers always knew the answer to that question.

FINDING ALTERNATIVES TO LAYOFFS

Promising no layoffs was the first step toward a labor partnership. There was still the challenge of how to manage the workforce when business dictated a slowdown in demand and less production work to be performed. Don and his team responded to these challenges with creative assignments for each worker. These assignments included concentration on product quality improvements, production efficiency, plant safety, housekeeping, and any other current operational problems that needed attention. This was truly a partnership based on mutual trust and respect.

In reflecting on how common layoffs had become as a way of managing the workforce during economic downturns, it is amazing to find how many other corporations have instituted a no-layoff policy. A simple Google search of "no-layoff policy" reveals many companies that had adopted such a policy. Among these companies were well-known brands such as SAS Institute, GoDaddy.com, Lincoln Electric, Publix, and Wegmans Food Markets. These companies had obviously made a commitment to their workers to avoid the costly psychological and economic damage caused by layoffs. They also appear to operate with great success. In 2013, Lincoln Electric earned a pretax profit of over one hundred million dollars. The company has had eighty years of uninterrupted profits, and this has been accomplished with a no-layoff policy dating to 1948. It would be interesting to learn more about how these companies have dealt with work slowdowns and how their bottom-line profits have fared under their no-layoff policies. We suspect they would tell us they have seen the same success that GM saw at the Tonawanda Engine Plant when workers were given job security.

Skeptics or opponents of a no-layoff policy will always raise the following two questions. The first is, "How will we manage costs during a business downturn?" The second is, "What will we do with the workers when we can't provide jobs for them during a business downturn?" We have addressed the first question already: redirecting workers' talents into maintenance, quality control, and other areas within the plant fulfills an ongoing need for these services. In addressing the second question, answers are more difficult because alternatives are fewer. We do know we don't agree with the strategy of one foreign car manufacturer located in the U.S. which pays its workers while on layoff. To us, this sounds like some kind of government welfare. It does not address the needs of the worker to be involved in meaningful work. This is not only a financial issue but one of self-worth and being valued.

LOOKING FOR SOLUTIONS TO THE LAYOFF PROBLEM

We have discussed this problem of layoffs with other manufacturing executives, and they are always quick to point out that this problem is not solvable. Rather than confronting the fact that they have ignored this problem far too long, they will often come up with all kinds of hypothetical outcomes to prove their point that layoffs are inevitable. Missing in their argument is the devastating cost of industrial warfare and the untold personal tragedies endured by the thousands of workers who have lost—and will continue to lose—their jobs and livelihoods.

We do not fault GM and other heavy manufacturing companies for seeking new and better ways to get improved financial results. Financially healthy companies benefit all their stakeholders. Recently, there has been increased recognition that organizational culture plays a large role in the financial health of a company. Recognizing the importance of organizational culture, GM has announced that there will be a culture change in its business. This initiative is a good step forward, but we believe there will be no significant culture change in GM, or anywhere else in manufacturing, until the problem of job security is first settled. We believe job security comes only when the layoff problem is solved.

So where do we go from here?

It is not our intention to solve the layoff dilemma here. However, we would like to suggest a few ideas for consideration. Businesses have invested tens of millions of dollars in forecasting demand for their products and generating models to control costs and waste in their production. Yet, in the case of economic downturns, very little planning and very few resources have been invested in how to minimize layoffs. We believe businesses have enough historical data on economic downturns to create a model of when they might expect the next one. If they can project slackening demand for their products, the next step is for them to prepare several operating plans ahead of time so that they can react successfully to different levels of severity or longevity during an impending downturn. Such a plan might well reduce the kinds of slowdowns or product changes that lead to job reductions.

Reflecting on the experience at the Tonawanda Engine Plant, we have evidence that the plant was able to successfully navigate through business cycles and changeovers without layoffs. We can state with confidence that it is possible to create job security and harmony in the workplace. And, we don't see unemployed GM workers walking the streets of Buffalo, New York, today.

Another step that management could initiate is a joint union/ management task force committed to finding an acceptable solution to what happens when business falls off and cost containment becomes essential to the survival of the company. One activity this task force should engage in is to visit other companies that have successfully implemented and sustained a no-layoff strategy. These companies, some of which were mentioned earlier in this chapter, should be viewed as models for "best management practices" in solving the layoff problem. In a recent *Fortune* article on great places to work, nineteen companies were listed as having a no-layoff policy. The number of employees represented in each of these nineteen companies ranged from a low of 1,142 to a high of 147,760. It is hard to believe that these companies don't face the same business cycles of our economy that auto manufacturing companies face. At the same time, these companies are known to be among the most successful in our economy. Perhaps they are just managed better.

The task force should also search for ways of insourcing parts that are currently outsourced. There should be many creative ideas coming from this task force that will address this problem. We believe the task force should also review the steps that are taken when employee cutbacks are inevitable. How can the company handle this with compassion? One example might be to offer workers early retirement, allowing them to use their pensions to support themselves and their families.

We don't want to do the work of the task force here; we just want to illustrate the kind of challenges the task force would need to incorporate into its mission. As a final challenge to the task force, it should present its complete statement of findings, conclusions, and recommendations to the top management of GM and the UAW, including the GM board of directors. Change will require cooperation between GM and the UAW.

Perhaps GM can take a lesson from how financial advisors approach investments in their clients' portfolios. Most financial advisors caution investors to avoid putting all their assets into one company or industry. The prevailing wisdom is to diversify investments in order to reduce the risk of any one failing investment causing a financial crisis. This strategy can also be applied to the automobile manufacturing industry.

Diversification can include acquiring companies in industries that are countercyclical to auto manufacturing. What this means is that a company like GM could create a diversified group of companies that would help it to manage business cycles, thus taking the pressure off any one industry group it owned to carry the burden of the overall financial health of the company. This could also mean that layoffs might be averted as a method of managing financial risk. We are aware that some companies have tried this strategy and failed. But we are also aware that Warren Buffet has created a portfolio of diversified companies, Berkshire Hathaway, that has been one of the major financial success stories in our lifetime.

In conclusion, if GM follows its stated commitment to change its company culture, it will need to address the challenge of layoffs. A complete and total culture change that will survive market volatility must include a minimal disruption to GM employees, both salaried and hourly.

Many other opportunities are likely to bubble up if management takes seriously its responsibility for retaining employees in times of lower sales and follows up with a serious intent to initiate meaningful employment. It is far past time to treat this subject with the sincerity it deserves.

CHAPTER 15

Making Work Interesting

Lots of jobs in the world challenge workers' imaginations and pique their interests from day to day, but there are also jobs that, by their very nature, are so monotonous and downright boring that you have to wonder why any worker would want, much less enjoy, such a job. More often than not, the factory worker did not select such a job but was assigned to it by some level of management. It is not implausible that some workers might tolerate such a job for any number of reasons. It might be that the worker finds such a job free of stress and perhaps easier to master than other jobs. Workers have also been known to actually doze off but continue to perform whatever level of work their job required. In those cases, the work is usually highly repetitive in nature and doesn't require much decision-making. The auto industry, by tradition and efficiency of production, generally requires a large number of such jobs.

A MODEL FOR ENRICHING FACTORY JOBS

For decades, behavioral scientists have studied the problem of how to improve boring, repetitive jobs. At Yale University, the work of the late J. Richard Hackman and his colleagues summarizes both the theoretical and research findings about how to make jobs more interesting and perhaps motivate the worker to perform at a high level of productivity. Hackman focused his attention on the work itself, identifying the qualities of jobs that make them inherently meaningful and motivating. His job characteristics model describes specific ways to design and enrich jobs. For example, by reversing the trend to simplify work and instead adding a variety of related tasks to a job, Hackman has shown how it is possible to change a monotonous job into a more interesting one. Also, by relating one's job to its final product, workers can see the connection between their contribution and the product more clearly, giving them a greater sense of accomplishment and pride. And, by reinforcing the significance of each job, workers will have the opportunity to see how relevant their contribution is to the final product.

Two other design characteristics to Hackman's findings are "feedback" and "autonomy." By feedback, Hackman referred to the importance of giving workers information and support so they can improve their performance. Knowing one is doing a good job is an important element of job satisfaction. Autonomy refers to the freedom of the worker to initiate activities that enhance work performance. This is contrasted by the limited autonomy that assembly line workers have in making changes to improve performance. Hackman's work is summarized below in Table 15-1. In addition, studies conducted mostly in Europe have demonstrated the positive effects of work groups created to reduce repetitive work and thereby boredom. By allowing more interpersonal communication, the effect of work groups appears to be improved worker attitudes and stronger personal satisfaction with work.

SUMMARY OF JOB ENHANCEMENT RESEARCH FINDINGS

CHANGE IN WORK	PRACTICAL EXAMPLE	DESIRED CONSEQUENCE
Task Variety	Add More Activities	Longer Work Cycle
Task Identity	See End Product	Pride in Work Output
Task Significance	Understand Contribution	Feeling of Relevance
Feedback	Knowledge of Performance	Improved Performance
Autonomy	Add Planning and Inspection	Strong Work Involvement

Table 15-1

The attempts to improve job interest at the Tonawanda Engine Plant paralleled the research findings just summarized and involved the initiatives discussed below.

USING TEAMS TO IMPROVE JOBS

One of the more successful efforts that GM management initiated in some work centers is the application of "teams"—essentially the same as the work groups described earlier. A team might be formed in an area where the jobs are similar or are related to the major subassembly being produced or even the final product. A typical team might have anywhere from five to ten workers, and they are all cross-trained in all the jobs they are collectively responsible for completing. This allows team members to rotate activities on a regular basis throughout the workday, thereby relieving some of the boredom. The team concept also encourages more communication and personal support for their teammates among the members of the team. Teams were given the authority to stop the subassembly if they detected a problem or a defective product. This gave them a level of autonomy that they were not able to experience working independently in the larger assembly line.

The team concept requires some level of discipline throughout the workday, and this responsibility is usually worked out among the members of the team. Teams were expected to resolve any communication problems they encountered. They were also expected to assist in developing proper procedures involving quality or any updated training that would be required in assembly of the product. An interesting byproduct of the team concept is that there is less demand for supervision or oversight, and this independence may have served to reduce the daily stress on the job. Combined, these work teams incorporated many of the features of the job enhancement research listed in Table 15-1.

IMPROVING JOBS WITH TECHNOLOGY AND INFORMATION SHARING

Technology also played a role in making work more interesting at GM. Many of the work stations were equipped with computer-controlled machines. Workers were trained to program and monitor the computers, thus involving them in the planning and ongoing quality control of their work output.

At one point in the early years of the auto industry, it was not considered important to keep the workers up-to-date on what was happening at the management level. At GM, it became prohibited for management to share any of the day-to-day data on financial performance, new product designs, or any operating strategies that were in effect—or even any that were planned. It was understood that this information was highly confidential. This secrecy on the part of management had become a constant irritant for the workers, who wanted to be included and to know more about their company. While GM offered some relaxation to the confidentiality of operating data, it was still not being shared at any kind of acceptable level to workers.

A major effort was undertaken to improve communication with workers away from the job sites. In an effort to help the workers handle day-to-day job stress, some level of daily communication flowing from the first level of management, as well as regular communication channels from all other levels of management, was planned.

GM's experiments at the Tonawanda plant were thought to be somewhat risky at first, but feedback from the workers led the company to expand its thinking on the subject of good employer/employee communications. GM was dealing with about 4,500 workers at the plant in the 1980s and early '90s, so it was a challenge to find a way to really upgrade communication efforts between management and workers within the plant. It was Don's decision to personally conduct a quarterly meeting with all the workers at which he would report performance data from all critical production lines. It didn't take long to find out that putting volumes of numbers up on a screen in the conference room, if not presented right, would also become boring for the workers.

One of the subjects presented in detail was the quality of the engines being produced. Workers were always interested in the report on any field warranty problems that had arisen associated with the engines they had produced. They all knew from firsthand experience that any customer with one of their engines would not be very pleased if that engine did not perform as expected.

Considerable time was spent discussing GM competitors and their success in the marketplace. It took a long time for everyone to accept the fact that it was not going to be possible to load all the competitors' cars back on the ships for a return trip to whatever country they had come from. On one occasion, Don wanted to demonstrate what he thought should happen to the millions of foreign cars that were arriving at U.S. ports daily. He showed a video depicting those cars being driven off the ships. He stated to everyone in the room that he would prefer the next section of the video, and he then ran the video in reverse, showing the cars going back onto the ship. That brought him a standing ovation and certainly generated some further conversations out in the plant after the meeting.

It was impossible to get all the workers into a conference room at once, so the sessions were limited to three hundred workers at each meeting. This meant that Don had to schedule three meetings per day for five consecutive days just to reach everyone. It was taxing to get that done every quarter, but the feedback was so positive that Don and his team made those meetings a high priority. They even added a feature by inviting the UAW chairman of the shop committee to become a partner in every meeting. This was a huge improvement for everyone. Over time, management became very comfortable with sharing its information with the UAW officers. Needless to say, this openness was well accepted by the workers.

THE POWER OF COMMUNICATION

The plant management had developed some hard and fast rules regarding what was said at those meetings. One rule was that lying to the workers on any subject being presented was absolutely forbidden. There can be no level of faith, trust, and respect for the workers if any of the data being presented were untrue, or even suspected of being untruthful. Another rule was to allow time for questions from the audience. This included time for giving complete answers or, if required, following up with answers at a later time and place. Another important rule was to never offer criticism to a group if the criticism was meant for one person. These rules were intended to build trust and openness while being sensitive to the need for workers to be treated with respect.

There were times of levity in these meetings, too. Don always told the workers that he hoped they would all be paid well enough that they could drive a Cadillac to work every day. They all knew he didn't make the decisions on what their pay grades were, but they liked the idea that he could jest with them about it. Somewhere along the line, the subject of GM bonuses came up. Other manufacturers, such as Ford, offered its workers a higher bonus at year-end if certain corporate financial goals were met. In the next round of meetings, Don brought up the subject of bonuses for discussion, and there was some concern among the workers about that. To bring that discussion to a conclusion, Don told the workers that his goal going forward was to be able to present all of them with a bigger bonus than the Ford workers got.

Well, it never happened before Don's retirement, and they never let him forget it. Eventually, they did get more—substantially more—and Don took pride in believing that something he had initiated while active at GM finally came to fruition after he had left: workers finally got the bonuses they deserved. They were the most outstanding workforce Don had ever had the pleasure of working with, and, to this day, they are still outstanding, with one of the finest engine factories in the world.

Another form of communication came directly from Don, as the top member of management at the plant. It was a high priority of his to spend as much time as possible out in the plant with the people who were doing the work. On almost every day, he tried to schedule a walk somewhere in the manufacturing and assembly operations. On those walks, he tried to acknowledge all the workers on their jobs. Often, one of them would signal that they wanted to talk. Don knew that you never want to intentionally move on in these instances or in such a way that might send the message that you don't have time to give them your attention. Sometimes workers just want to know that you care enough to spend a little time listening to what they might have to say, or perhaps even ask a question about their job. It never hurts to inquire about their family or some other item of interest they might want to bring up. These conversations helped workers feel engaged and relevant to the entire operation of the plant.

There were other ways to let the workers know they were appreciated. For many years during the December holiday season, poinsettias would be brought into the plant for every department. It wasn't unusual to see a beautiful poinsettia plant riding down the line on an engine saddle for all to see. No, this wasn't a big thing, but it was a way to let the workers know they were always on management's minds and that they were appreciated. On some occasions, boxes of chocolates were delivered to every department, and, yes, they would be seen going down the assembly lines, too. In retrospect, these ideas were essentially monotony breakers, and at least they provided a way to make days more interesting.

One other significant effort to communicate with the workers and make their work more interesting was the regular publication of the plant newspaper. It was published by one of the UAW members who participated in the public relations aspect of the plant's operations. It contained messages side-by-side from union officers and management, and it became very useful in announcing events and presenting information to the workers that might otherwise not have come out in normal everyday activities.

Sometimes it is so easy to overlook little things that might be very important to the workers. You have to live and learn in the culture-change business, but you never want to give up. Culture change, once entered into, is a one-way street. There is no turning back, and it can be one of the most rewarding efforts that management will ever undertake.

On a final note, Don learned that making work more interesting for the workers must never be treated lightly. In fact, it may well be one of the most important efforts undertaken to bring culture change into the operation. There is no greater lesson than learning that any management success in changing culture is directly proportional to management's success at inviting workers to become real members (Don and his management team always referred to them as "partners") of the enterprise and share in whatever successes are generated by that enterprise. Don and his staff felt strongly enough about their partnership with GM's workers that they actually had a box of business cards created for each worker with his or her name printed on it and identifying each of them as partners in the operations at the Tonawanda plant.

Don and his team had neither asked for nor obtained GM's approval for that effort, but they were never criticized for it, either. There were those outside the plant who would have worried that the UAW might attempt to use the word "partner" as a lever during contract negotiations, but Don's management team had very high respect for its UAW partners and trusted them to enjoy the partnership identity of the workers. And they did. It is unfortunate that other divisions of GM never adopted the Tonawanda Engine Plant's policy with the UAW, which came to be called "Partners in Progress"; based on the success he had seen with it at the Tonawanda plant, Don knew it was a missed opportunity when GM failed to embrace it elsewhere within the company.

In another chapter, we will present one of the most unusual activities that Don and his team ever envisioned for the workers at the Tonawanda plant: the start of the Chevrolet Employee Sales Team. In that effort, Don saw the real power of a culture change. It was the ultimate effort to make the plant's workers' jobs more interesting. What Don did not anticipate was that the effort would be adopted across most of GM's operations and become a major contributor to the company's sales and marketing strategies.

This chapter was devoted to how the content and context of work can improve workers' interest in their jobs. The initiatives described in this chapter were designed to offer more intrinsic enhancements to the plant's work by using teams and changing the job routine to reduce boredom and repetition. More autonomy and flexibility were added to the workers' control over production. Teams allowed more social interaction, while increased communication from management helped build a stronger relationship to the whole plant and its performance. Management did not shy from addressing worker issues. In fact, they solicited them with the intention of taking action whenever possible. And finally, the little things that showed management's appreciation, such as the Thanksgiving dinners and holiday poinsettias, went a long way in letting workers know they were part of the GM community. Humor and levity became part of the culture because workers felt at home and engaged.

The Tonawanda Engine Plant had become a great place to work!

CHAPTER 16

Extending Work into the Community

In the mid-1980s, the Tonawanda Engine Plant was tooling up to produce the new engines for the introduction of the Chevrolet Corsica and Beretta cars. Don and his team were concerned about how successfully those cars would sell when they hit the dealers' showrooms. Having been through recent failing models, the team knew that the quality of the engines they produced was only one factor in the successful launch of a new car model.

Part of the open communication initiative with workers was to share management's concerns about the success of the company. The team spent many hours discussing its concerns with workers and getting their thoughts on the table. Everyone knew that the long-term future of the plant was directly tied to these engines doing well in the marketplace.

It became very obvious to both management and workers that the quality in the production of the new engines would be tantamount to the public's reaction to the cars when they drove them. It did not escape anyone that the quickest way to turn off customers was to have them take delivery of a new Corsica or Beretta with an engine that did not perform up to their expectations. With that in mind, Don and his team pondered what else they could do at the plant level to add some zip to the sales of these new models. How could they assist the plant's local dealers to get the public more interested in buying these new cars? From these discussions, a plan came into focus. It was called the Chevrolet Employee Sales Program.

THE CHEVROLET EMPLOYEE SALES PROGRAM

In reflecting about this unique initiative, Don wondered whether it would be possible for everyone who worked at the Tonawanda plant to get involved in the sales and marketing side of the automobile business. In all honesty, it did seem a little far-fetched to find a way to cross that boundary between production and marketing. To his knowledge, nobody else in the manufacturing side of the business had ever tried it. The first thing Don needed to find out was whether the workers would be interested in such a program. He arranged meetings to gauge their interest. To his surprise, the workers thought it was a very good idea. They were eager to help in any way they could.

To ensure cooperation, Don met personally with both Al Warren, head of GM labor relations, and Don Eplin, president of the UAW, to obtain their approval and buy-in. They both gave their complete support for the program. This was critical because these activities were not part of the labor agreement, and both GM and the union needed to give their support.

Don wondered how the local dealers would react if the engine plant workers suddenly exhibited an interest in their business. One of the plant's local Chevrolet dealers, Paddock Chevrolet, thought it was a grand idea and offered to help set up the program. The first obstacle to be overcome was to provide some kind of sales training for everyone at the plant. To help organize the training, union officers got involved in laying out a simplified plan. To many, the notion of the union working with GM management on this initiative seemed incredible. But the union leadership had grown to trust management, and what would seem like the impossible became a reality. Workers embraced this new role without commissions, incentives, or other compensation. The Chevrolet Employee Sales Program was clearly a breakthrough in management/ union cooperation.

News traveled fast. Several young executives from GM headquarters had heard about the program. It was unusual for headquarters to get involved in internal plant programs, and that the news of the program had made it back to headquarters was a welcome surprise. Corporate management was very helpful with suggestions in how the plan would work.

When the plan was finalized, attention turned to implementation. Everyone was encouraged to look for new customers for the new Corsica and Beretta cars. Employees were enthusiastic to contact everyone they knew who might be ready to look for a new car. This included neighbors and relatives who were high on the list to contact.

Don knew it was important to add some recognition for everyone involved in the program, so he had a jacket specifically designed for workers with the words "Member, Chevrolet Sales Team" embroidered on the back of it. Anyone who made a sale with the new car delivered through a dealer would get his or her jacket at a special ceremony in the plant. The dealers were very accommodating in helping deliver the jackets to make sure the appropriate recognition would be given for each sale.

What happened next was quite spectacular. Sales were taking off. At first, the workers were focusing on the Corsica and Beretta cars, but as momentum grew, the program was opened to all GM cars and trucks.

One problem that surfaced early was a concern by some workers who were worried about their customers experiencing a problem with the car they had sold them. This concern led to an enhancement to the program. Each employee who had made a sale also had to stay with his or her customer until any engine problem they may have experienced was solved at the dealership level. This essentially committed the plant employees to car maintenance and making sure that customers received the best service possible. Going one step further, Don, with the support of the entire plant personnel, added to this enhancement by selecting a few very experienced engine mechanics to help with any difficult-to-diagnose engine problems. These mechanics were already working in the plant, and now they were being made available to local dealers as needed. This turned out to be another positive because the plant would get an early warning if any problems surfaced in the new cars, allowing engineering to come up with an early solution if necessary.

The jacket award meetings were most interesting. They were scheduled as often as sales necessitated them. One very special Chevrolet dealer, Duane Paddock Sr., was always available to present the jackets to the salesperson for each sale. It wasn't long before people would see the plant's GM workers/salespeople out in public, proudly wearing their new jackets. The jackets attracted lots of attention. Some workers were more successful than others at finding customers and closing sales. On many occasions, employees would come to Don's office and with excitement let him know they had gotten their first customer. For Don, those were the rewards that really counted. They were etched in his memory as evidence that the sales program was really important to workers. It was evidence that plant workers indeed wanted to do more to help the company to succeed than just build its engines.

It was a little later in the program that workers started paying attention to what were labeled "conquest sales." These were sales in which an employee had convinced a potential customer that GM cars were a better choice than whatever they had been driving. There was a great deal of pride shown when a conquest sale took place.

At one point, Don realized that an important segment of the workforce, the Security Department, had been overlooked. Security personnel were invited to participate in the program by pushing sales of the Chevrolet police cars. These employees were not to be outdone by anyone else in the plant. They readily took on their phase of the program and worked very hard at it. They contacted every police department they could find and presented not only their sales pitch but added informative meetings to present engineering details unique to the Chevrolet special lineup of cars designed for police work. Over the next few years, they had actually covered most of the police departments in the State of New York and delivered literally hundreds of cars. It was hoped the police officers driving those cars, while handing out traffic tickets to the public, would not give the plant too much publicity for providing them with state-of-the-art police cars that really helped them with their law enforcement responsibilities.

As the employee sales program gained success, other GM plants began to start their own sales activities, and over time the program actually spread across most of GM's plants. On one occasion, the president of GM invited a group from the Tonawanda Engine Plant to GM headquarters for a sales recognition meeting and photographs. Nothing close to that had ever happened before, and it brought cheers to the workers at the plant.

To recognize the workers' contributions to making the sales program a success, a special day and event was planned for all the employees. At this event, a full set of business cards for everyone in the plant—identical to the one shown for Richard Houghtling—was handed out. The face of each card clearly stated the employee's name, identifying them as business partners in the Chevrolet Employee Sales Program. The reverse stated the plant's quality policy.

It wasn't long before those cards started showing up all over Buffalo. Now, all employees became more visible in their travels, exhibiting their jackets and offering their business cards to one and all. Even after thirty years it is not unusual to spot someone wearing their sales jacket or handing out one of their sales team business cards. It was certainly evidence that it is always a good idea to give the people who do the work a chance to display their talents and accomplishments.

Over the following years, the sales program literally sold thousands of new cars. The success of the program far exceeded any expectations that may have existed when the program was first conceived and launched.

It must have resonated in the high offices of GM in Detroit because the Tonawanda Engine Plant is still prospering after all these years. The plant's reputation for innovation and employee involvement did not go unnoticed. Today, when GM designs a new engine, the Tonawanda plant is usually first in line to produce it.

This might be a good place to reiterate what had been accomplished with the Chevrolet Employee Sales Program. As we have stated in other chapters of this book, the people who do the everyday work of producing engines deserve to be treated with faith, trust, and respect. We believe this program was instrumental in demonstrating the positive response of the workforce to management's confidence in them and their confidence in management. This reciprocity of positivity is what allowed Don and his team to innovate and succeed in enhancing the role of workers into an area where they had never ventured. Don and his team believe they lived up to their workers' expectations with this program, and Don and his team can state categorically that the workers exhibited the same level of faith, trust, and respect toward plant management as it had in them initially. Together, we have seen what can happen when labor and management take it upon themselves to act in accord with what would be a "Partners in Progress" business strategy. We will have more to say about this strategy in a later chapter.

THE CHEVROLET TONAWANDA CAR SHOW

Along with continued success with the new engines in the early 1980s, Don was looking for ways to make working at the Tonawanda plant more interesting for everyone. One of the suggestions that came from the ongoing dialogue of how to add more visibility to the work being done in the plant was the possibility of organizing a public car show, right in front of the plant. It was thoroughly discussed with the union officers and workers, as well as the management team. There was consensus to proceed

and make it happen. Don had always wanted the local dealer organization to be involved in activities that would be of significant interest to their dealerships. With the help of some local car show planners, a task group made up of managers and workers selected a time and place for the first show. It would be on a weekend in the end of June, when the plant would be entering its annual changeover and temporary shutdown. Invitations were sent to local car show enthusiasts with the rules for entering their cars.

To make the show as interesting and relevant for GM workers as possible, the rules required that all show cars would have to display an engine that had been manufactured at the Tonawanda plant. Everyone involved was pleasantly surprised at the interest shown by the community. The number of cars on display and the larger-than-expected turnout of visitors were testimony to the success of this program. To top off the day, judges selected the best of show cars and awarded their owners trophies when the day ended.

The reaction from workers was great. They enjoyed showing off the products they had a part in manufacturing. This program also helped to reinforce the strong focus and ever-increasing attention to the quality of the products being produced in the plant.

As a result of the success of the plant's getting into the car show business and the cooperation with local dealers, it was decided to continue the show on an annual basis. As the years went by, the show became more prominent, growing every summer. It became so popular that the show was opened to restored cars of all makes and models. It was not unusual to see cars show up from other states and Canadian provinces. What started out as a low-key local car show evolved into an international event that attracted new and restored show cars and large crowds of people. This far exceeded the modest success that the original planners had hoped for.

The Tonawanda Engine Plant version of car shows was so successful that it was continued for the next twenty-seven years. It may never be known how large the impact was from a business perspective, but it sure made working at the Tonawanda Engine Plant a lot more interesting.

Workers took great pride in showing off the plant and the engines they produced. The community also benefited as evidenced by the size of the attendance at the shows. And over the years, it was not uncommon to have the plant win best in show for appearance of the main plant and its manicured front yard. Visitors were often seen taking their cameras out to capture what a modern manufacturing plant should look like in a community.

In summary, both the Chevrolet Employee Sales Program and the car show are examples of how extending work beyond the factory and into the community led workers, their union, and management to cooperate and bring a sense of pride to the workplace. The energy and innovation that went into these programs are also evidence of the lifting of the industrial depression that had plagued the plant and the complete transformation of its workers into a highly motivated workforce that was a true partner in making the plant and its products exceptional.

CHAPTER 17

A Passion for Excellence

Most, if not all, manufacturing enterprises claim to produce their products at a high level of operational excellence. Survival in the manufacturing business may well depend on manufacturing excellence. What is not well understood is what it takes for a manufacturing operation to become excellent. Many have learned much about quality from the work of W. Edwards Deming, the founder of the "Total Quality Management" program and author of the famous "14 points" on quality management within organizations. Others have also witnessed the results of product and process excellence programs in several Japanese manufacturing companies, most of which were embracing Deming's quality principles.

Unfortunately, GM was not a quality leader; in fact, it was perhaps a lagging follower in creating programs to improve manufacturing excellence. In this chapter, we will describe how the Tonawanda Engine Plant adopted not just a program to improve quality but also a passion for excellence. We will give examples of the changes that helped to shift the plant culture from accepting mediocrity to significantly improving the quality of its products and manufacturing processes.

DEFINING PASSION FOR EXCELLENCE

Excellence does not just happen by sheer coincidence, accident, or good luck; it starts with the leaders of the organization. Their credibility must be impeccable. They must exhibit a quality of leadership that builds confidence in the entire organization. A workforce that trusts its leaders is a workforce that can be counted on to perform at the operational excellence level.

A passion for excellence is not something that is inherited. It is created by example and, like a virus, can be infectious. It can be transmitted from one leader to workers and from worker to worker. Although contagious, its benefits do not occur immediately and completely within an organization. A passion for excellence needs to be nurtured and evolve over time. With very few exceptions, it is the recipe for increased job satisfaction and improved quality of work life. Once it catches on, this passion is an intense, visible, emotional drive to perform an operation at the highest attainable levels. It is highly doubtful that this level of passion for excellence can be attained without a strong culture to support it.

THE CASE OF HARLEY-DAVIDSON

Examples are all around us to help demonstrate what a passion for excellence is all about. We have chosen one organization as an example, the Harley-Davidson Company, to illustrate how a passion for excellence can transform a company.

Why Harley-Davidson?

The reason is simple: it had succeeded in transforming its corporate culture. Before the sale of this company to new owners, Harley-Davidson was a failing company. Its products were of poor quality, and the company was losing market share to Japanese and European imports. Since the takeover, Harley-Davidson has accomplished a complete turnaround. The new leadership dedicated itself to a corporate strategy of creating products with flawless engineering, quality, performance, durability, styling, and reliability. As a result, the demand for its products has exceeded the supply, resulting in the company being able to sell its products at a premium price.

In recent years, a demographic shift has challenged Harley-Davidson to appeal to a younger generation that is less enthralled with motorcycles than past generations. However, we believe they are an excellent example of how a change in culture can transform a company, contributing benefits to all its stakeholders, while increasing its sales and profits.

If Harley-Davidson is so highly successful, why aren't more companies or corporations attempting to do the same thing? We believe the answer, most likely, is that most other organizations lack the leadership and drive to get it done. Further, we believe that most organizations are content with making a profit, and excellence for them takes a back seat to a positive income statement.

To the credit of the Harley-Davidson Company, its passion for excellence has helped it stay on top of its industry. A company staying on top of its industry can be more difficult than getting there in the first place because it requires an acute understanding of what its customers are looking for in a product. It requires that the company design and implement an effective manufacturing process and create an organizational culture to support its processes. It requires a flawless marketing strategy for its products. The company's customers demand continuous improvements, regardless of their high level of satisfaction with existing products. Success has not diminished the company's need to continuously improve and deliver the best products possible.

What has excellence contributed to Harley-Davidson stockholders? It is public knowledge that Harley-Davidson stock has appreciated substantially since the management buyout took place.

While its financial success is outstanding, many of its other features are common throughout its industry. This is a company whose employees are represented by the UAW union. The company pays the usual union-scale wages, and it provides the usual benefits. The company is not subsidized by any kind of government funding.

While all these features are similar to other companies in its industry, the most identifiable characteristic that sets Harley-Davidson apart from most other companies is that it operates with a passion for excellence.

An example of how Harley-Davidson has embraced excellence is embodied in the changes it made in 2009, during a sales decline. With the full cooperation of its two unions, the Harley-Davidson plant in York, Pennsylvania, completely redesigned its operations to truly create a new, modern factory. The company converted a formerly dark, dingy manufacturing environment into a clean, automated factory driven by continuous improvement. In an *IndustryWeek* article, Ed Magee, the factory general manager, stated, "Work was getting done, but it was not a world-class manufacturing environment. We wanted to create a sustainable, lean culture."

Within the four walls of its lone manufacturing building in York, roughly one thousand production workers now fabricate, paint, and assemble motorcycles in three process areas with a system simplified by automated, guided carts. The conveyor belts transporting parts through the painting process that once stretched nine miles through the plant are now just three miles in length. Robots now rhythmically weld parts together—and do so faster and more precisely than before. The plant churns out 20 percent more fenders per shift than in years past and does so with two fewer employees.

In this flatter organization, workers now have one of just five job classifications, a notable change from the sixty-five classifications used under the old framework. The new factory in York also now relies on flexible workers to supplement its leaner workforce. During what it calls its "surge period," the company ramps up its production by 50 percent and brings in a bevy of flexible workers to work side-by-side with full-time hourly employees.

The Harley-Davidson success story was not lost on Tonawanda Engine Plant employees who invested in a new Harley. This included Don, much to the surprise of many employees and UAW officers. It became popular for many of them to gather for a weekend of fun, riding as a group to destinations of mutual interest. The photo above shows one group ready to depart the plant together. Don can be seen on the white Harley on the left at the head of the group.

CREATING A CALL FOR EXCELLENT QUALITY

We would like to shift our attention back to GM. In 1983, when Don became the plant manager of the Tonawanda Engine Plant, its workforce was in a state of industrial depression. The engines the plant was producing were of poor design and quality. This created tension and finger-pointing, but little progress was made in improving quality. Things were so bad that the top GM executives in Detroit were ready to close the plant. The skeleton workforce that had been decimated by the recession had fallen victim to the same malaise and feeling of helplessness that permeated the entire work environment at the plant.

Recognizing that the plant could not survive in its current state, Don and his management team created a plan to turn around its failed culture. One of the critically necessary cultural changes Don identified at the Tonawanda Engine Plant was to instill a sense of pride, both in the workmanship of the products and the processes that produced them. Don knew this was necessary if the plant were to eliminate poor quality. Attention was given to matching specifications with blueprints, creating systems that would enhance product reliability, identifying causes of poor quality, and redesigning those products that did not live up to quality standards. But most importantly, developing workers' skills so they could deliver high-quality products was Don's highest priority. Don knew that without investing in the most important toolset of all—the skill of the workers—the quality of products would always be limited by the skills of the workers producing them. Worker development required more than just training; it had to include how the workforce was treated and integrated into the process of creating high-quality products.

The cultural shift to excellence at the Tonawanda Engine Plant was a challenging undertaking. The workforce included more than four thousand employees over most of Don's tenure as plant manager there. Don knew it would be naïve to think that the plant could operate for long periods of time without any product quality defects. It can be safely said that there was never a day that went by that the plant did not experience an internal machine problem or a supplier product that did not perform satisfactorily in assembly operations. And, yes, some quality problems were attributable to an employee who had made a mistake of some kind. But Don knew he had to recognize that even the best employees, being human, can make mistakes. He needed to be sensitive to how he treated mistakes so that he did not alienate workers from the very process he was trying to create.

GETTING THE MESSAGE OUT ABOUT EXCELLENCE

There were times when Don would be asked to make a presentation about engine quality to upper management or other interested personnel, either inside or outside of GM. Being aware that not everyone in any given audience had the faintest idea of what was inside a finished engine, Don devised a way to clarify what it takes to produce a quality engine that would perform to a customer's expectation. His presentation went something like this:

A typical V-8 engine, ready to be installed into a car or truck, contains upwards of five hundred separate parts. Each part has to meet complex quality requirements, whether produced in-house or at a supplier plant. For illustration, let's look at one of the eight pistons. It might be made of aluminum, or it could be some other material such as cast iron or even some kind of steel. If that piston were to operate on a stroke of four inches, then for each revolution of the engine, that piston would travel eight inches in the cylinder bore. If the car or truck were to be driven with the engine rotating at two thousand revolutions per minute, then each of its eight pistons would be traveling about 1,330 feet in its cylinder for each minute that the vehicle maintained that speed. In one hour at that speed, each piston would travel 79,800 feet in its cylinder. If the vehicle were to hold that speed for a normal eight-hour day, each piston would travel 638,400 feet in each cylinder—the equivalent of about 121 miles.

That is just in one day of operation and one piston in one cylinder. Put into the customers' perspective, where they might expect to own and drive that vehicle for one hundred thousand miles over several years, each piston would be required to travel over 25,000 miles in its cylinder. In other words, each one hundred thousand miles the car travels over the road is the equivalent of four trips around the world, and each piston in its cylinder would travel the equivalent of one time around the world. By this calculation, the combined eight pistons will need to travel two hundred thousand miles in their cylinders. This is accomplished with only a thin coating of motor oil separating the surfaces of the pistons from their cylinder walls. While the pistons are doing all the traveling, the other five hundred components in the engine must perform at the same level of quality. This level of quality can only be accomplished within a culture that supports a passion for excellence. It was the GM Tonawanda Engine Plant's goal to accomplish this level of quality with every engine it produced.

On one occasion, Don was told that a corporation in Oklahoma had three Chevrolet Suburbans that were used to transport people from a city to a distant airport, and each of those trucks had 850,000 miles on it. He was told that the trucks had only had normal maintenance performed on them at regular intervals. Don offered the company three new engines in exchange for their used ones. The company was more than happy to make the trade. Back at the Tonawanda Engine Plant, Don's team disassembled those engines and found that there was so little wear on the pistons and bores that they still passed through the tolerance gauges successfully. The owner of those trucks happened to be a well-known oil company, and it claimed it was their oil that allowed the engines to perform so well. The real story here is that, first, the engine has to be built at the highest standard of excellence before the customer takes delivery, and, second and equally important, the engine must receive outstanding maintenance.

Then, and only then, can the engine deliver such outstanding performance and reliability.

THE CHALLENGES OF OUTSOURCING

GM did experience quality problems from its suppliers from time to time, and it became a critical issue as the demand for higher levels of quality were required in its products. Over time, Don was able to work with most suppliers to develop more and better control of the quality of their products before they shipped anything to the plant. Suppliers were to understand that the plant expected the shipments of products it received to be free of quality problems of any kind. As the years progressed, Don was able to buy and install measurement systems into the plant's machinery that would shut down operations upon identifying a faulty part. This capability allowed the plant to more rapidly meet or exceed its customers' demands for quality and reliability. Today, the technology being designed into manufacturing machinery at the Tonawanda Engine Plant is far superior to anything Don had employed in earlier years. But one fact is clear: the tradition of building excellence into the manufacturing system continues to pay dividends for the plant today.

QUALITY VERSUS POLICY

Sometimes, striving for excellence runs counter to existing corporate or plant policy. Don experienced this firsthand in an unusual situation where quality was one of the challenges as the plant prepared to order towing tractors to be used by its material-handling people. These tractors would only be used to tow trailers of material to the assembly lines. At that time in the 1980s, Don's direction to the plant's purchasing staff was that the plant would not purchase manufacturing equipment from Japan. It was part of GM's effort to keep Japanese products out of its plants. GM knew that Japanese companies would try to take over everything possible to have a larger role in its business.

But when GM's purchasing department investigated potential suppliers of the new tractors and eliminated from consideration any that were made in Japan, the purchasing staff was not completely satisfied that it could find a domestic supplier with the capability to meet the requirements being sought. Don decided to invite plant employees into the discussion to see whether they might have some ideas or suggestions. Don was not surprised that they welcomed the idea of helping to purchase the tractors they would ultimately have to operate. Don's direction to them was to go out to the tractor suppliers and find the best tractor for their use. Employees loved this assignment, one of the first that had ever allowed them to get involved in decision-making. In due time, they reported their findings.

When they met with Don, they told him they had found the supplier that offered the best tractor, but they seemed to be holding some information back. After questioning them further, they admitted that the best tractor available was one built by a Japanese manufacturer. This posed a dilemma because those workers felt even more strongly than Don that they did not want to purchase tractors from Japan. Don's answer to them was that since they were going to have to use those tractors, they would have to decide what course of action to take. They came back very soon with a proposal. They had told the tractor supplier that the plant would purchase their tractors, but only if all brand identification on the tractors were removed.

Don realized right there that these workers valued good quality ahead of principle and any objections he might have. In fact, perhaps they had made quality the most important principle underlying their decision. Don couldn't argue with that. He told them to proceed with the purchase, but the tractors would require close inspection by the workers when they arrived. Don reinforced a belief he had always held: never underestimate the ingenuity of the people that do the work, and support their decision to embrace quality over corporate policy.

The decision to purchase Japanese products at that time would not have been approved by GM top management. Don, believing that quality trumped policy, forgot to make GM top management aware of this purchase.

ENGAGING WORKERS IN KEY DECISIONS

Don learned it isn't always obvious how manufacturing decisions will have a large impact on in-plant product and operating quality. In the mid-1980s, when GM had been awarded two new engines for the Corsica and Beretta cars, the Tonawanda plant was one of the first to purchase major machine tools offshore. At that time, the plant needed to have a new kind of flexibility designed and built into its new equipment. New equipment needed to have the capability to provide a wider variety of functions. The plant's domestic machine tool suppliers had not yet started building such flexible types of machines. These machines would need to be designed and built in such a way that GM would be able to change them over very quickly to produce new products, thereby greatly reducing the lead-time to get products to the marketplace.

The plant found what it was looking for in Italy and ordered at least three major machining lines to produce aluminum cylinder heads. The Italians were more than pleased to accept the plant's orders, and they excelled at getting the machines built and ready to be run off and tested at their facilities. The run-off test was an opportunity for GM staff to visit the Italian operations to critique the new equipment while it was machining test products. It was also a good opportunity for GM personnel to learn as much as they could in a few days on how the equipment would need to be installed at their plant. The proper installation of the equipment was critical to the finish quality of its product at the end of the machining.

While Don was meeting at the Tonawanda plant to prepare for the trip to Italy, he realized he had a crucial decision to make: it was normally members of GM management and engineers who would attend the runoff. This time, Don decided that it would be a very wise decision to send some of the plant's skilled tradesmen.

After all, these were the people who would ultimately install and set up the new equipment. The visit would give them a head start in their planning as the machines were being delivered. With that in mind, Don invited many of his skilled tradesmen to an in-plant meeting to work out the installation plans. They had never been invited to a machine runoff, even at other GM plants in the U.S., so they did not expect Don's well-timed final question.

"Would any of you guys be interested in making the trip to Italy for the runoff?"

A sea of hands filled the air. In fact, they were almost ready to race home and begin packing. It was obvious to Don that the plant could not send everyone, so he asked the plant's UAW officers to help select the most qualified tradesmen for that assignment.

After the new-style runoff was completed with tradesmen present to see the equipment function and ask questions of its manufacturers, the machinery began to arrive at the plant. It was installed in record time and without any of the major problems that usually accompany such a large project. In the years following the start-up, this new equipment performed in a way never seen at the plant. It produced the highest quality products ever and did so at an all-time high level of up-time. In earlier projects involving the introduction and assimilation of new equipment, the plant would typically generate a level of up-time (the percentage of acceptable products per hour of production) of roughly 50 percent. This new equipment reached a level of daily up-time that reached all-time highs of up to 90 percent. This was a remarkable breakthrough that would reduce the number of machines the plant would need for future projects. Once again, Don learned that placing your faith, trust, and respect in the people who do the work is a very wise investment of your human resources.

There are many more stories of Don's success with his efforts to instill a passion for excellence and quality in the Tonawanda Engine Plant. His experience in changing the culture showed that with planning, employee engagement, and a supportive management style, almost anything can be done. There can be no question that management and workers alike embraced a passion for excellence.

GM would be wise to look closely at the changes made at the Tonawanda Engine Plant; these changes created one of the strongest, most cooperative labor/management partnerships in the auto industry. It is a plant that demonstrated how a risk-free atmosphere for making new investments in engine manufacturing operations can yield exceptional results. By demonstrating what is possible when a passion for excellence replaces industrial depression, the plant flourished. For Don, one thing is clear: the plant's new approach took GM through a much-needed culture change.

CHAPTER 18

The Bully Manager

In the world today, there is much discussion on the topic of bullying. More often than not, it is a topic that arises involving youngsters and schoolchildren. One child may exhibit tendencies to overpower another child with aggressive behavior. These activities can be in the form of hurtful words or, in more serious cases, physical contact. The result can cause the recipient of bullying mental or physical trauma.

Our interest in this subject is limited to the kind of bullying that takes place between members of management and members of the workforce. We have labeled managers who engage in bullying behavior "bully managers." For the purposes of this discussion, we will define a bully manager as someone who is habitually cruel to others who may be in a lesser organizational role or perceived to be weaker. A bully manager may try to dominate, browbeat, intimidate, or heckle others. One of the most pervasive forms of bullying can often be found at top management levels.

149

Both authors have witnessed bully management in the workplace. While we will be taking a close look at this management style only at the Tonawanda Engine Plant, we believe this style is pervasive, and even accepted, in many organizational structures, including industrial, military service, academic, and professional settings. In his recent memoir, *Hillbilly Elegy*, J.D. Vance observed how uneducated, low-skilled workers have animus toward educated people because those are the people they typically interact with at work and who treat them poorly, often bullying them. Bullying by those in power has a profound impact on those who are dependent and vulnerable. This is clearly played out in traditional manufacturing environments and particularly in unionized auto factories. The seeds of hostility and its toll on productivity can be found in these environments.

DEFINING BULLY MANAGEMENT

Managers are granted authority, by common law and tradition, to oversee the work of others. How this authority is put into practice is a major contributor to the culture of the organization. Authority can lead to bullying behavior and tactics that force the will of those in power onto others. The use of threats, aggression, and discipline by managers can lead to intimidation and fear among their workers. The reaction by those who are subject to bullying may vary from compliance to contempt. The natural tendency of bullied workers is to defend themselves through avoidance and seeking protection. In the case of auto workers, the UAW was the chosen protection, although this union is limited in protecting workers from day-to-day bullying behavior that has become the norm in most auto plants. The recipient of bullying will be defensive and distrustful. Much of the discussion in earlier chapters is testimony to the negative culture that follows from bully management.

An alternative use of authority is to engage the worker through faith, trust, and mutual respect. This management style is sometimes called "servant leadership." Rather than using forceful tactics to get workers to do their jobs, servant leadership views authority as less important than including workers as partners in the organization's effort to be successful. Under servant leadership, managers call themselves "servant leaders" and view their role as helping workers by providing them with the resources they need to perform their jobs. This includes training, coaching, joint problem-solving, and the tools and equipment they need to be effective. Servant leadership, as suggested by the title, entails the manager serving the worker and avoids bullying.

It is surprising how often bully managers will try to blame someone or something else for their inability to get results. A bully manager does not engage in analysis and problem-solving to improve performance and will not seek cooperation or a partnership with workers to resolve workplace issues. Bully managers project their negative attitude toward workers by using authority and coercion in an attempt to get what they want.

Unfortunately for them, this rarely works.

CONSEQUENCES OF BULLY MANAGEMENT

The lack of trust and respect for workers under bully management is a major contributor to industrial depression, described in Chapter 10. When bullying is pervasive, as it was when Don took over the Tonawanda Engine Plant, industrial depression had spread throughout the plant, even to workers who had not directly experienced bullying. It was like a virus: infectious, contagious, and with no known cure. The personal damage that was inflicted on workers was devastating. Their quality of work life was seriously damaged, and their alienation from their work environment was manifested by high absenteeism, frequent grievances, passivity, poor quality of work, lack of energy, and a strong distrust of management.

Let's look at a few specific examples of bully management in action.

One example Don observed was from a plant manager in a large GM plant. This plant manager seemed to enjoy using abusive language when he had subordinates gathered in a meeting room. He particularly zeroed in on a specific mid-level manager every chance he got, and over a short period of time this manager gave up trying to hold a conversation with him and gradually withdrew his efforts to do a good job. The manager had been on a fast track to higher levels of responsibility, but he ended up resigning prematurely. He died shortly after leaving his job. The bullying plant manager finished out his career as a vice president and was never held accountable for the human damage he had caused to this mid-level manager.

Another supervisor was famous for berating workers in front of their peers. The types of incidents that provoked this behavior were not wearing prescribed safety equipment, reporting late for work, returning late from a break, or not following mandated operating rules. While these infractions deserved attention, it was the public reprimanding that was humiliating to the worker. By embarrassing workers in front of their peers, this supervisor gained the disdain of all his workers.

Alan and his colleague Mike Gent, while consulting with one of the engineers at the Tonawanda plant, witnessed an event that became etched forever in their memories. The engineer's office was enclosed in glass. Without warning, a high-ranking supervisor began pounding on the glass, causing the glass to shake. He was shouting for the engineer to come out of his office, angrily pointing an accusing finger at him. The consultants were embarrassed for the engineer and shocked at the behavior of the supervisor. The engineer had a stellar reputation and had been assigned to the project that Mike and Alan had been working on. When he returned to his office a few moments later, he apologized for the incident. It was obvious from the look on his face that he was humiliated. Alan and Mike excused themselves to let him recover from what had been one of the most bizarre cases of bullying they had ever seen.

ELIMINATING BULLY MANAGEMENT

Faced with a plant infested with bully management as the dominant leadership style, Don was challenged with how to eradicate it. He knew that bully management had to stop if he were going to change the culture of the plant. He started his eradication efforts at the top, with his general superintendents, and continued down through all the levels of supervision and, ultimately, to the shop floor. Don made it very clear that he would not tolerate bully management. He shared the features of his servant leadership style and encouraged his team to engage workers, seeking cooperation rather than co-optation. He emphasized this at every meeting he held. In short time, everyone in management got the message. However, while those closest to Don embraced his new management style, some resisted it.

These were supervisors who just could not or would not change. In servant leadership, they perceived the loss of authority, real or imagined, as untenable. This resistance required a difficult but necessary decision by Don and his team to eliminate a whole level of management. Radical as it seemed, the clear message to both management and workers was that Don meant business. As a result, workers became more conversational with management. A flatter, more responsive servant leadership management structure brought workers closer to their leaders, and they became more involved in solving work-related problems. Finally, the ice was broken, and a new era of cooperation between management and workers had begun.

It is worthwhile here to point out that you can never exhibit true faith, trust, and respect in and for your workers without totally and completely eliminating bullying from your management style. Bully management is antithetical to a culture that is built on mutual respect and trust. In fact, bully management will kill any attempts to build a strong, supportive culture based on mutual respect and trust. As Don learned firsthand at the Tonawanda plant, it just doesn't get done that way.

CHAPTER 19

Holidays in the Workplace

MAKING HOLIDAYS SPECIAL

One way to understand an organization's culture is to observe how it celebrates holidays and special events. At the Tonawanda Engine Plant, the management team thought that national holidays presented opportunities to create a special occasion event for all employees. A closer look at two holidays shows how the plant approached celebration with the entire workforce.

On Thanksgiving, Don decided it would be uplifting to have the managers organize, staff, and serve a full-course Thanksgiving dinner to all the workers. To spice up this event, all the managers who were servers would be dressed in chef's uniforms and hats. There were many expressions of surprise and appreciation from the workers before, during, and after the dinner. Don was sure that the plant had reached a significant emotional milestone in its workers' quality of work life.

But not so fast!

A few days later, a group of workers came to Don's office. This usually meant some kind of problem. However, Don soon learned they had come to his office to let him know how much they had enjoyed their Thanksgiving dinner, but they said they didn't really feel right about it because they knew there were hundreds of disadvantaged men and women down at the Buffalo City Mission who might not get a nice Thanksgiving dinner at all. Don knew immediately that he had overlooked something important in his planning. The word went out to the plant that Don understood the workers' concerns, and in the future not only would the plant continue its plans to serve meals on special occasions, but it would first send a thousand meals over to the City Mission. Everyone was pleased with this decision. Don learned a valuable lesson about the plant's workforce: it appreciated celebrating but also expressed empathy for those less fortunate.

Another favorite holiday in the plant was during the Christmas season. The plant normally would shut down for a week or more at that time, which included the New Year's Day activities that were always scheduled in the local communities. The last day of work before the holidays began was quite a special day for everyone. The workers were allowed to bring in their favorite foods, groups of workers from all over the plant would gather together at lunchtime, and a holiday feast would take place. Management was invited to share in the activities. With regard to this celebration, two important conditions had been approved in advance by both the UAW representatives and management: it was agreed that everyone wanted to enjoy the day, but there could be no alcoholic beverages brought in with the food. The second condition was that the plant still needed to meet the day's production schedules. The workers met both conditions, and they went out of their way to make sure at the end of each shift that the workplace was clean and tidy, with no sign of a celebration having taken place. Overall, it was a day to remember for everyone, and they left for their holiday vacations with a good feeling about the plant and their employer, GM.

In preparation for the holidays, Don also tried to make things interesting on a day-to-day basis. As described previously, in Chapter 15, the plant would bring poinsettia plants in for every department to brighten the work sites. Don also wanted to let the workers know they were being remembered. On other days, the plant would send boxes of Christmas candy out to all the departments. It was fascinating to watch the interest when Don sent a few boxes of candy right on the conveyor, down the main assembly lines. What a difference it made in the work areas when everyone was drawn into the celebration, especially when the plant announced the events in advance.

OTHER WAYS TO CELEBRATE

Sometimes, the celebration simply involved taking pride in the plant. Workers took a strong interest in making the plant look good. One activity that stood out was dressing the lawn in front of the plant with flowers and shrubs. The workers were interested in having the local community recognize the excellent landscaping. The plant even won contests acknowledging the beautiful appearance of its grounds. In one year when the budget was tight, workers actually participated in planting flowers and grooming the lawn. As shown on page 158, there was little doubt that these workers enjoyed making the plant attractive.

Other signs of celebration were more spontaneous. Many workers had organized bowling teams, and on bowling night these workers wore their bowling shirts to work. And, when the Buffalo Bills or the Buffalo Sabres were playing, workers often wore team clothing.

Don could go on and on about how workers in the plant expressed their enthusiasm about holidays and special occasions. None of this could have happened if management had not shown its faith, trust, and respect for the workers in the plant.

CHAPTER 20

The Bottom-liners and Culture Change

In this book, we have presented the case for how the culture of a company affects every aspect of its existence. We have shown how a negative culture can lead to dysfunctional behavior, which, in turn, leads to an increased cost of doing business. And, we have shown how improving the culture not only leads to a better work environment but also improves communication and cooperation at all levels of the organization. In large organizations like GM, decisions tend to be made at corporate headquarters and handed down to its divisions. Because GM divisions produce products but do not sell anything, the effectiveness of each division is measured to a large extent by its costs. If corporate headquarters is driven to increase its bottom line—that is, its profits—the effect at the divisional level is to lower costs wherever possible. One consequence of this bottom-line thinking is to view investing in culture change as an expense. We believe that placing profits as the top priority will drive out any significant investment in culture change. It is ironic that one of the biggest drains on profitability is a negative culture.

In his book *Culture Trumps Everything,* Gustavo Grodnitzky compared the overall performance of public companies that represented "classic capitalism" with public companies known to favor "social capitalism." The difference between classic and social capitalist companies is that the former focus primarily on financial returns to owners, represented by the share price of their stock, whereas the latter show a balanced approach by serving multiple stakeholders, including owners, employees, customers, suppliers, and the community. Grodnitzky's data show that his list of social capitalist companies significantly outperforms classic capitalist companies, and this disparity grows bigger over time. Grodnitzky calls this "the profit paradox"—that is, those companies that strive for profits as their top priority are less profitable than those that serve multiple stakeholders. It is noteworthy that Grodnitzky's sample of social capitalist companies includes three automakers, none of which are U.S. companies.

Most of the social capitalist companies in Grodnitzky's comparison had been identified by Rajendra Sisodia, David Wolfe, and Jagdish Sheth in their book, *Firms of Endearment.* The authors give many examples of how these companies treat employees with respect, often paying higher wages, offering better benefits, and providing a more flexible and supportive work culture. The success of social capitalist companies is more evidence that a positive culture is an investment, not an expense, contrary to what proponents of classic capitalism may argue.

DRIVERS OF BOTTOM-LINE THINKING

Why are corporations like GM so bottom-line driven?

Much has been written about this. Our American economic system rewards investing in companies that are profitable. Executives are measured and rewarded on the bottom-line profits of their company. These executives are often rewarded with stock options. It is in their self-interest to drive up the value of their company stock. And, there is the tyranny of a stock market that judges the value of a company's stock by the strength or weakness of its earnings. The least drop or change from expected profits can have a severe impact on the stock's value and the net worth of the executive who is being rewarded with bonuses for increasing profits and often further compensated with stock options.

This sets up an interesting dilemma for corporations. If profits and the way executives are rewarded become the primary corporate objectives for success, other stakeholders, such as employees, vendors, customers, and the community where the corporations reside, will be poorly served. There is little debate that GM has a long history of ignoring the real needs of its workers: pressuring vendors to cut costs, often at the expense of quality; producing poor-quality products or products that do not meet customer expectations; and abandoning communities and plants in pursuit of lower costs. It is little wonder why GM went from commanding over 60 percent of the domestic auto market in the 1950s and '60s to clinging to less than 20 percent of the market today.

PUTTING AN END TO BOTTOM-LINE THINKING

We believe the only way GM can change its culture is if it abandons its bottom-line mentality in favor of a balanced stakeholder model. The focus of this book has largely been on GM workers. It is shocking to us that the people who do the work are not a high priority to the management whose success is dependent on these workers. The fractured relationship between management and labor at all GM plants has resulted in huge costs to GM. It is even more shocking to realize that GM largely ignored this problem, fueling further deterioration that led to even higher costs.

GM is not alone in its pursuit of profits as its primary goal. Of all the priorities to be considered, it is very rare to find any industrial organization that doesn't consider profit to be the very highest priority. We understand how and why corporations exist and therefore why profits are important: they are an excellent measure of the financial health of a company. It is profit that makes it possible for any business to grow and expand. It is profit that makes it possible for a business to pay wages to its employees, issue dividends to stockholders, and create a return on investment to its bond holders. It is profit that makes possible the corporation's ability to pay taxes to the many and varied facets of government that keep communities and the country running.

Our concern is that profits are often viewed only in the short term and pursued at the expense of other important stakeholder outcomes.

Years of observation and research on culture change brought us to the conclusion that if you are a top manager who thinks profit, or the bottom line, is priority number one, you have bypassed your greatest opportunity to bring about real success to your organization. We refer to these managers as "bottom-liners." The remainder of this chapter will be devoted to how this bottom-line thinking can impede efforts to change culture and how this bias can be overcome in an effort to bring about true culture change.

We have found that some business leaders or top managers may have a real interest in a culture change for their organization but just haven't been able to make the decision to go forward. Sometimes, it is just the level of risk or fear of the unknown that holds them back. They know that once the decision to go forward is made, there is no turning back. Or, they may have trouble finding just the right time or triggering event to set the stage for the kickoff that will convince the organization that a culture change is necessary. There may also be a fear that a culture change could cost real money and in some way jeopardize their bottom line. Nothing scares a top manager more than an unanticipated hit to his or her budget. In light of these concerns, culture change may never take place, and the opportunity to become a truly great business will be lost.

To successfully change a culture requires major changes in behavior at every level of the organization. Most managers would love to change the behavior of workers, but unless they are willing to change their own behavior, culture change is not likely to happen. Psychologists will tell you that behavior change is difficult. Sustained behavioral change at all levels in an organization is even more challenging. New behaviors must be continuously reinforced until they become habit. Otherwise, people will fall back into their old behaviors and defeat any chance of positive change.

IT STARTS WITH BELIEVING IN PEOPLE

We have argued in earlier chapters that developing faith in people by earning their trust and respect is necessary for real change. In our experience, the lack of these critical beliefs about people is a major obstacle to culture change. In the most severe cases, where managers do not recognize that their employees are an important and valuable asset, there will be little or no interest in culture change. In these cases, we would recommend a serious look at changing the leadership of the organization. Culture change requires leaders who can be the role models for the behaviors they want to establish.

It has been interesting to watch the dynamics of GM's most recent effort at reorganization, following the company's bankruptcy in 2009. GM promoted Mary Barra to be the new CEO, and, recognizing how deeply rooted the company's problems were, she pledged to change its culture. It was a very difficult time to take over a massive corporation that had recently declared bankruptcy and was about to deal publicly with a major ignition switch problem that had reportedly resulted in deaths and caused a large-scale, costly recall that would bring with it significant organizational changes. It was refreshing to hear that GM would face up to the blame for its quality problems and vow to once and for all make all corrections that were required.

On Friday, June 6, 2014, *The Wall Street Journal* published the headline, "GM Takes Blame, Vows Culture Shift." It signaled that one of the most responsible and, yes, "breathtaking" organizational behavioral changes in the history of GM was taking place. Time will tell the rest of the story, but there is no indication at the time this book is being published that there has been any softening of the resolve at all levels of GM to get the job done. In fact, we see new reports of improved product quality, productivity, and positive financial performance already. That is exactly what one would expect when a business makes a sincere declaration to change.

Intentions are fine, but intentions alone will not ensure a lasting culture change. To transform a culture, a major investment needs to be made in leadership. Leaders will need to become change agents; they will need to make major investments in listening and instituting changes that promote positive attitudes and a can-do orientation toward problem-solving. This is contrasted with the more traditional approach to push and direct people rather than engaging them as partners in the production of automobile parts. At the Tonawanda Engine Plant, Don witnessed the beginning of a new life for the worker. It is not unusual to hear workers who used to say, "I hate getting up to go to work there," now saying, "I look forward to going to my job every day now." Yes, a positive culture is a powerful motivator of people.

The kind of change we are talking about cannot happen in a bottom-line-oriented company. To establish a positive culture, a "means/end" test must be part of the formula for success—that is, a positive organizational culture is the means to the end result of long-term profitability. A negative culture is costly, and no matter how hard management tries to increase profits, this culture will drain the resources of the company.

One way to view the development of a positive organizational culture is as an investment, with the "return," or payoff, being the release of positive human energy. A positive culture makes it possible to generate human energy in pursuit of organizational goals. In the long run, this will lead to a healthy bottom line. It is sad that so many businesses never harvest their human potential, wasting their opportunity to be great. And even worse, bad cultures either suppress human energy or release it in a negative way.

Job security is and always has been a top priority for industrial workers. And yet the typical bottom-liner never gives a second thought to the effect of layoffs on each worker who is told on Friday afternoon that his or her services are no longer needed in the immediate future—and in many cases, will never be needed again. Layoffs are personally devastating and a misused business strategy. GM's strategy of laying off workers at the first sign of a drop in sales or profits was a major reason for the industrial warfare that has plagued the company and cost it billions of dollars in lost productivity.

An engaged workforce will always outperform a workforce that is part of an organization infected with industrial depression. You can demand improvements in productivity, efficiency, and profit, but what you get will never match the free-flowing, spontaneous energy that comes with a positive culture. It is highly unlikely that you will find an engaged workforce existing in a hostile environment, unless the workers are simply engaged in resistance against those whom they see as responsible for the hostile environment.

Some believe it is impossible to create a positive, cooperative culture with a unionized workforce. Yet, the transformation of the Tonawanda Engine Plant demonstrated how a major business setting where the workforce is organized can be changed. In this case, a toxic culture changed into one of the most positive cultures that could be offered to both management and union personnel. This change did not take away or interfere with the activities generated by the union. In fact, it enhanced the opportunities for the union leadership to represent its members in supporting the partnership between management and workers.

Once an investment in culture change has been made, it may take years before it has matured to a level where it is sustainable. Having reached this level, it can survive through the inevitable challenges that businesses face, including recessions, technological advances in both products and manufacturing, and changes in leadership and the workforce. A strong, positive culture can support any corporate strategy—except one: *there is simply no way to accommodate a bottom-line-first strategy within the positive organizational culture we have been advocating in this book.*

CHAPTER 21

Setting the World Record

One of the rewarding consequences of the culture change at the Tonawanda Engine Plant is the willing participation of the workers in new and different activities that make their work more exciting and rewarding. Such an event actually took place at the Tonawanda plant several years after the plant was rewarded two new engines for the Chevrolet Corsica/Beretta program.

Don was operating the plant on two ten-hour shifts to keep up with demand for the two new engines as well as the other engines already in production at the plant. In a staff meeting, a question was asked about how many engines the plant was tooled-up to produce on a daily basis. On an average day, running two eight-hour shifts, the plant could expect to produce about 6,500 engines. And, on a day with two ten-hour shifts scheduled, it could get that number up to eight thousand engines, provided there were no significant operating problems. Don wondered what the plant's maximum output might be if the workers went all-out to test their ability to produce engines.

The idea of a special production day was suggested and discussed with everyone in the plant, including the union officers. It sounded interesting to everyone, and Don and his managers began to put a plan together to meet this challenge. They picked a day, one when they were sure they would have enough material on hand to meet whatever the demand turned out to require. It would be a day when everyone would help build engines, no matter what their regular job may have been. This was a major decision because it had been unheard of for management to be allowed to help the workers on the production line. It was also a departure from contractual rules to allow any management personnel to actually participate in the assembly of engines. It was the one day when the plant manager would not only be allowed to work on the lines but was actually required to do so by everyone in the plant.

On the appointed day, Don arrived at his usual starting time before 6 a.m., the normal starting time for the production lines. The union officers were waiting for him with the job they selected for him to do. They escorted Don to their big V-8 engine line. His job was to be assembling a very heavy cast iron flywheel onto the rear of the crankshaft. It required starting six bolts into the two parts. When the first engine came to his position, Don had the flywheel in place and began to start the six bolts, but he was interrupted by the loud voices of the workers behind him on the line. They were yelling that Don was holding them up, and he interpreted this to mean he should get himself moving a little faster.

The union officers standing to his rear made no attempt to help or quiet the yelling; in fact, they seemed to be enjoying Don's predicament. When the second engine came to his position, the union officers told Don he just wasn't qualified for such a skilled job and took him to another location in the plant. That's the way the day went. The workers were having a great time, the union officers were busy helping solve any problems that came up, and the managers were all finding out what it was really like to actually be responsible for the assembly processes. When the day ended, no one knew what the final engine production counts were. The plant would not find out until the next morning.

It was obvious that there was excitement in the air as Don arrived the next morning. As it turned out, the excitement was well justified: while the plant's tool capacity was 7,040 engines per day, the plant had produced 8,832 engines in one day. Don had done some homework before, and he knew what the capacities were for some of the larger engine plants in the world. He was quite sure none of them could outperform his plant at 8,832, so the plant decided to claim a new world record for the most engines produced in one day. That record stands to this day. There was only one challenge about setting a world record, from Volkswagen, but its production was not even close to the number of engines the Tonawanda plant produced on that day.

With a great deal of pride, Don decided to let GM headquarters know of the event, now that it was over. Don was reasonably sure that GM would, in all probability, not have allowed such an endeavor, especially since it involved the crossing of contractual lines of demarcation between management and the union. Don decided that the best way to notify GM was to send telegrams to the current CEO and president announcing what the plant had accomplished. Surely, they would want to join in the recognition of anyone setting a world record in one of their plants, right?

It turns out Don was wrong about that.

Shortly after Don had informed the GM top executives about the world record, he received a call from GM's CEO. The CEO only wanted to know whether Don had spent any extra money on that day to build so many engines. Don assured him that the plant had only worked the same hours that it had been scheduled to work. Furthermore, because the plant had built so many engines on that day, those engines were the least expensive that the plant had ever produced. Don's conversation with GM's

CEO was short and soon over, with no other questions or comments. When the CEO finished his call, the GM president was waiting for Don on the other line. He wanted to know whether the plant had any unusual quality problems while producing so many engines in one day. Don took pleasure in informing him that the day had been one of the best ever as far as quality was concerned and, further, that there were no engines waiting for any kind of repair at the end of the day. After he had hung up, Don realized that he had just talked to two of the top officers in GM, and neither the CEO nor the president had shown any sign of sharing in the pride that he and his management team and his workers felt in setting a new world record. Clearly, the top brass at GM had little in the way of faith, trust, or respect for the people who had worked so hard to make this day happen.

What do you do after setting a world record and the dust finally settles? Don could let everyone in the plant know what he now knew: beyond all doubt, the Tonawanda Engine Plant possessed capabilities that were far beyond those of any other engine plant in the world. Don was aware, however, that the record-breaking day was special. Don was concerned that the union officers and workers might see the special day as a precedent for ratcheting up output for normal production days. Any attempt at this would be the quickest way to deflate the morale of the entire plant, destroying the trust that had been carefully nurtured— clearly, not a good idea!

Don never tried to leverage any kind of new performance expectation based on the phenomenal success of that day. He and the workers celebrated those results as a wonderful day in the big plant—one that everyone could enjoy and be proud of.

Upon reflecting on this special day and the world record that was set, Don realized how far the plant had come from the days of industrial depression and poor morale. He was struck at how it was possible to make what is typically a boring and monotonous job of bolting engines together into a more interesting kind of day—the kind of day when all who worked at the plant are anxious to get up and go to work. It can be the kind of day when you want to go home and tell your family about your day at the plant. It is the kind of day when you can be comfortable, knowing that you can trust management and that you can place your faith in them to have your best interests in mind as they make plant operating decisions. Finally, there is no substitute for being able to earn the respect of the workers who come to the plant each day to work. The relationship Don had nurtured between workers and management was a two-way street, with faith, trust, and respect being conveyed from management to workers and from the workers to management.

This is a good time to have a discussion about a very important subject that has plagued many corporations and businesses over the years. In the last chapter, we touched on the fact that a great many top managers seem to judge their success by the bottom line of their operations, and so we have conferred the title of "bottom-liners" on them. It is our firm conclusion that a true bottom-liner will very seldom enjoy the level of success that Don achieved at the Tonawanda Engine Plant. To bottom-liners, the workforce is merely a means to their real goal of maximizing profits. Lowering costs at the expense of the workforce is very much a strategy to be profitable for these managers.

The irony is, as we have demonstrated in this chapter, the managers who place a higher priority and emphasis on treating their workforce with faith, trust, and respect will in most cases end up with greater success than those who allow the bottom line to dictate their decisions. This is a concept that may be a bit hard to swallow for the bottom-liners, but there are many examples of highly successful companies, both locally and across the country, that are living examples of the truth in our concept. As a final observation to back up our concept, we can point out that the Tonawanda

Engine Plant is not only alive and well, but it is one of the most modern and productive plants of its kind that you will find anywhere. The plant is producing many of the state-of-the-art engines that are found in current GM automobiles and trucks, including the new Corvette engines. We feel confident in claiming that the culture change that took place in the Tonawanda plant over the past twenty-five years is mainly responsible for its current and ongoing success.

If our readers are wondering, the world record set by the Tonawanda Engine Plant stands today. There have been challenges, but no engine plant has come close to matching the world record.

PART FIVE:
SUSTAINING CULTURE CHANGE

CHAPTER 22

Why GM Needs to Change its Culture

We have tried to bring into focus, in a forthright way, a synopsis of the auto industry, from its beginnings, through its growth, and on to the state of the business as it is functioning today. From its inception, the auto industry showed great promise in the United States. It produced much-desired transportation products and created jobs for a country that was rapidly growing and changing. The industry provided the stimulus to grow the economy of the United States into the largest and most influential in the world. There is no question about the enormous influence the auto industry has had in shaping the country.

However, with this influence came many missed opportunities, particularly in the manufacturing environment, where so many people were employed. We could have filled this book describing each missed opportunity for GM. Instead, we decided to identify and recognize the successful opportunities to improve and define the steps needed to fulfill the original promise the industry had offered. We believe it is not too late to take a serious look at the history of the auto industry, its successes and its failures, with the goal of implementing the changes required to fulfill its original promise.

While most of our attention is with General Motors, we believe the organizational culture of manufacturing plants at GM shares a remarkably similar history to that of other automotive plants with different owners, such as Chrysler or Ford. Over the years, if you were to have visited an auto manufacturing plant in this country and you hadn't actually seen the name of that particular corporation on the front of the building, you would have been hard-pressed to decide which member of the auto industry you were visiting. The buildings were similar, and the machinery was in most cases identical and often supplied by the same vendors. In more recent years, even competing car models use parts from the same suppliers, often a competitor. Our point is this: although our focus is on GM, our observations and analysis can apply to any of the "Big Three" U.S. auto manufacturers—Chrysler, Ford, or GM.

A HISTORY OF INDUSTRIAL WARFARE

We have detailed some of the major problems of the auto industry, particularly at GM, although the same problems existed throughout the entire auto industry. In the years following the introduction of the assembly lines that bolted cars and trucks together, a serious management error occurred that has plagued the auto industry right up to the current time. Employees, the people responsible for doing the bulk of the work, have been treated as interchangeable, replaceable commodities—simply little more than another component of the assembly line. They were viewed as necessary to produce the cars, but they were not valued as human beings. Their jobs were repetitive, boring, and very demanding to keep up with the speed of the assembly lines. Working conditions were poor, hot in the summer and cold in the winter. But workers needed their jobs, so they put up with these conditions as long as they could.

In late December 1936, matters came to a head with the sit-down strike at the old Chevrolet Motor Plant in Flint, Michigan. It was there that history first witnessed how management could make an employee's life miserable—a capability that would repeat itself throughout the 1950s and '60s. It was there that a first-level supervisor was often measured by how many penalties he could dole out. It was there that top management practically ignored workers in its effort to produce cars more cheaply. It was there that the labor-management relationship began to deteriorate—until the day the Flint plant was closed forever.

As part of the settlement of the sit-down strike in 1937, the UAW was granted the right to represent auto workers across the industry. At that particular time and place, GM and the UAW could have come to an understanding of the obvious: that they were going to have to be partners, jointly involved in the manufacture of automobiles. They might have realized that there were two distinct paths they could follow: they could enter into some kind of "industrial war" or they could become "partners for progress" by management accepting the union as a true partner.

It is very sad that GM chose to battle the union and its workers, making one of the greatest management errors that has ever been made in the auto industry. Management took an intense dislike for the UAW and erected every possible roadblock it could dream up to deploy against improved relations. The UAW wasn't much better. The union used every tool at its disposal to protest management and its practices. What a shame that such major sources of energy on both sides were wasted fighting a never-ending industrial war that could never be won, a war that would weaken the industry and allow foreign competitors to gain a foothold in the domestic market.

It is also very unfortunate that the industrial war just described permeated the very top of GM and the UAW from the start. This negative relationship cascaded through the many GM divisions and plants that came along later. As an example of how badly conditions had deteriorated, the strikers blocked all the gates into and out of the plant during a particularly testy strike at the Flint plant. Members of management were seen getting into the trunks of cars in order to get through the gates without being molested by the strikers. From a purely human perspective, one has to wonder how a workplace relationship between management and labor could ever have deteriorated to that level of animosity.

INDUSTRIAL DEPRESSION AND LOSS OF ENERGY

Two of the key chapters that describe the sad state the manufacturing environment at GM had fallen to are "Industrial Depression (Chapter 10)" and "A Practical Discussion of Human Energy (Chapter 11)." Briefly, but as covered in detail in these chapters, when workers don't enjoy their jobs and working conditions are poor, they quickly become disenchanted and withdraw, detaching themselves from their jobs and the company. One of the results is that they no longer look forward to going to work. They continue to show up because they need their job to provide an income to meet their personal and family needs. A related result is that workers will withhold their energy, only doing the minimum of what they have to do in order to keep their jobs. They may also lose pride in their company and its products.

Consequently, when a workforce is allowed to deteriorate to that level, the enterprise that they work for will soon begin to see a decline in both product quality and financial stability; in fact, it will suffer poor results in just about every area worth measuring. Tragically, not many managers even recognize these real symptoms, let alone the causes, of industrial depression. And worse, they may not have a clue of what to do about it if they did recognize it. The good news is that there is a way to turn such a situation around, and that is what several of the chapters about culture change are about.

CONTINUATION OF INDUSTRIAL WARFARE

As we have previously stated, this book would not be complete without offering some resolution for the negative results the auto industry has experienced with its labor force. The UAW should be included in this discussion, but first let it be clear that we have no axe to grind with the UAW in this book. The UAW has competent, intelligent people who have capabilities beyond GM's expectations, but they have endured stunning setbacks along the way. A fallacy has undermined their strategies over the years, too. From the beginning, when negotiating with GM and the auto industry in general, the UAW would conjure up a myriad of demands that they would present to management as necessary and required to create a new contract or to settle some already existing problems. At that point, the two parties could come to some compromise and then move on to other business. All too often, instead of a mutually acceptable compromise on the part of both parties, either management would not acquiesce to their demands or the UAW would reject any compromise offer from management. In that circumstance, the negotiations would descend into a more hard-nosed—and less productive—confrontation on both fronts. The next step on the part of the UAW would be to threaten management with the possibility of a work stoppage unless the union was granted its version of a settlement. In retrospect, the UAW position would take on a likeness to "legal extortion" and an invitation to chaos. If current reports are accurate, this industrial war is still alive and well, with the most recent case of legal extortion underway regarding new demands from the union for profit sharing.

At this point, it is very difficult to imagine that a major industry and its union counterparts would not recognize the negative outcomes that would become byproducts of such a strategy. The foreign auto manufacturers must surely have thought the heavens were smiling on them when they were presented with such a vast opportunity to enter their products into competition with U.S. automakers. They must have recognized immediately that the domestic auto industry, such as it was at that time, was fraught with the results of so many wrong operating decisions. They knew that U.S. products exhibited major quality problems and that overall operating performance was well below where it should have been when U.S. automakers owned the entire domestic auto industry.

How could such a condition have developed in such a great country as ours?

Actually, it isn't hard to explain. The leaders of the auto industry and the unions were locked in battle and took their eyes off the real threats in the industry. Where were the boards of directors and top management personnel? Where were the union officers, who were elected to support workers? What was so attractive about keeping the costly industrial war alive for so long? Why did the unions not recognize the reasons why their foreign competitors always chose to build their factories in the South, in right-to-work states?

We find it very difficult to avoid using the words "arrogance" and "incompetence" when trying to answer these questions. When moving to a more current discussion of our nation's auto industry, people are often reminded that Lee Iacocca is credited with asking the mother of all questions: "Where have all the leaders gone?" Perhaps the answer could be that they were never there in the first place.

Before we move to a more current discussion of our auto industry and its unions, let's go back to the 1930s one more time, but come up with a scenario that just might have made a world of difference in where we are today. What if, at the end of the sit-down strike in 1937, management and the union had strategized a different path forward? Since both sides knew that they were both there to stay, the only logical conclusion would be that they must become partners for progress in the auto industry at some level. Had the time been taken for this realization to sink in, the industrial war might not have been initiated. Even today, after an embarrassing bankruptcy and bailout of the auto industry by the U.S. government, recent events have surfaced indicating that our nation still has a long way to go before its auto industry can once again assume the position of world leadership. Recently, it has been reported that GM executives withheld information about faulty ignition switches in GM cars that led to deaths and injuries. This led to a major recall, and litigation that is likely to go on for years.

In our opinion, it will take a significant culture change before GM can once again become a leading industrial company. To the credit of its current leadership in Detroit, there is a strong recognition that such a major transition may be forthcoming. The previously mentioned *Wall Street Journal* headline from 2014 certainly suggests as much: "GM Takes Blame, Vows Culture Change."

Maybe there is hope after all.

THE NEED FOR CULTURE CHANGE

When it comes to challenges confronting the auto industry, there are some big ones that will ultimately have to be recognized sooner or later. We have not seen much evidence that the auto industry is now treating its workers as though they were a valuable asset.

Think about that.

How could the industry not have faced that issue years ago? Its leaders are living under the absurd notion that it is just a normal and acceptable practice to treat the people who do your work as pawns in the high-stakes game of financial viability. They call it good management to lay workers off at the earliest indication of a possible drop in sales or reduction in profitability. Leaders of businesses that rely on the practice of worker layoffs can often be heard boasting about how they dumped their workers to achieve a miraculous financial uptick.

We would like to present a challenge to both management and unions. It has been Don's experience to have enjoyed a rewarding relationship with all the officers and the workers with whom he had the privilege to work during his long career at GM. The Tonawanda Engine Plant could never have accomplished the successes that have been spelled out in the preceding chapters of this book without the union's help. It is our firm belief that a strong working partnership between management and unions can accomplish great successes that would never have been possible while continuing to fight the industrial war.

Maybe it is time to bring an end to the industrial war that has been going on for so long in the auto industry and redirect some of those energies toward partnering with workers. Just think of the impact this would have on lifting industrial depression and releasing the energy that could be directed to strengthen productivity, improve quality, and enhance overall company performance. There are many smart people in the auto industry. It is time for them to start working together on solving one of the biggest obstacles to their industry's success.

FOREIGN COMPETITION AND STRATEGIC MISTAKES

When foreign manufacturers came for a business visit, it was not difficult for them to spot the weaknesses in the U.S. domestic auto industry. They proceeded to pounce upon the glaring opportunity they saw, one that would bring them across the oceans with their new products and strategies to compete with American products. The fact that they were able to implement their strategies right into the middle of the world's largest auto market is amazing. Since most of the major auto plants in the U.S. were located in the northern half of the country, foreign competitors decided to locate in the southern half of the country, in right-to-work states, where there was very little in the way of union efforts to organize labor. The foreign auto manufacturers paid attention to how the workers in U.S. plants were treated and responded by creating a highly visible positive culture in their workplaces. Not surprisingly, the workers liked what they experienced in these new plants and provided support for management's efforts to become strong competitors of U.S. car brands in quality, functionality, and price. U.S. auto plants were at a distinct disadvantage to compete because of the hostile management-union relations that characterized their ongoing industrial warfare with one another.

Although this book is about culture change, it is important to understand how GM failed in its business strategy. Clearly, we believe that its negative work culture and the corporate warfare between management and the UAW were a major strategic failure. Abraham Lincoln, in his famous June 16, 1858, speech against slavery, stated that "a house divided against itself cannot stand." These would have been wise words for GM executives to hear and embrace. The divisiveness between management and labor left GM vulnerable to competition by adding costs and reducing the cooperation and unity needed to fight foreign competition.

Call it arrogance, but GM executives looked down at foreign competitors, practically inviting them to enter the domestic car market. Most Americans viewed early auto imports as either poor quality, as in the case of Japanese cars in the 1950s and '60s, or too expensive, as in the case of higher-priced European brands. Veterans of the auto industry can recall the years when they started to see foreign engineers and managers visiting our country with cameras and notepads. They weren't just on a long-awaited vacation to our country; they had a very serious agenda, and they followed it to a tee. There were a great many executives in the auto industry who simply did not believe that foreign companies could ever break into their business, and, as history has shown, they never could have been more wrong. Foreign competitors spotted the weaknesses, as well as the strengths, of U.S. auto manufacturing, and they determined very early that there were some big gaps in how U.S. companies did things. Exploiting those weaknesses and filling those gaps would become their main focus in implementing a strategy to begin capturing what the U.S. auto industry always thought was "their" business.

Another reason it was relatively easy for foreign competition to enter the U.S. auto market is that foreign manufacturers focused on quality and price. In the initial attempts by the Japanese to sell their cars in the U.S., their cars were viewed as poor quality. Realizing this, they worked hard to improve their quality, while American manufacturers let their quality slip. Our chapter on the Caprice Fiasco (Chapter 12) provides a good example of how quality became secondary to the primary focus of the auto industry in the 1980s: meeting production schedules. It should come as no surprise that this was the decade that foreign competition accelerated into high gear. Foreign competitors also focused their sales on smaller cars with smaller engines. Most Americans preferred larger cars, but events in the economy dramatically changed this preference.

In 1974, American drivers experienced something they had never seen: severe shortages of gasoline and higher prices. When it was available, there were long lines to get gasoline. In some cases, there was rationing. This hit drivers hard, and they began to look for automobiles that offered better gas mileage. American cars were heavier and more powerful, guzzling more gas than most foreign cars, and thereby allowing the smaller, more fuel-efficient imports a competitive advantage in the sale of new cars. The response from American carmakers was too late and too weak. They had bet on cheap gas and were wrong.

Could cooperation between management and the UAW have allowed GM to be more competitive and successful in retaining the domestic car market? We believe this cooperation could have been a major force to effectively fight foreign competition. But it wasn't to be. Today, there are new challenges. But the solutions that were never applied are still viable: it is not too late to change the organizational culture to combat industrial depression, release human energy in a positive direction, and foster a whole new way of doing business inside GM's manufacturing operations.

CHAPTER 23

Summary and Hope for the Future of GM

During his nearly forty-year career at General Motors, Don was a change agent. The origins of his need to right the ship at GM were rooted in his small-town upbringing in a farming community in Minnesota. Here, Don learned the value of cooperation and teamwork toward a common goal. He also learned to respect all people, always seeing the good in them. He carried this positive attitude toward people to General Motors, first at the Flint Engine Plant and, with progressive promotions, ultimately to GM's largest engine plant, in Tonawanda, New York.

When Don first arrived at the Tonawanda Engine Plant, he was shocked at how much animosity there was between management and the union. As a superintendent, he took it upon himself to walk through the plant with a union officer, who showed him the problems that existed for workers. Don knew these problems were fixable and made sure they were taken care of the next day. Over time, trust grew between the union leadership and Don, which allowed him to engage in one of the biggest and most successful cultural changes in the history of the auto industry.

Don was promoted to the top job at the Tonawanda Engine Plant in 1983. Shortly after accepting this promotion, the top management at GM informed him that unless dramatic changes took place at the plant, it would likely be closed. Challenged by this, Don convened a team of managers and union officials and shared the news. He also expressed hope that, working together, they could save the plant. This meant winning new work from GM headquarters and signing a labor contract with the UAW. Don also knew that he needed to change the culture at the plant, eliminating the warfare between management and the union and offering the workers job security and a better work environment. Over the next few years, not only were Don and his team able to bring in more work but they also watched their workplace evolve into one of the most productive engine plants in GM.

How did Don do it?

He began with the most important issue that divided workers and management: job security.

Don made a promise to the workers at the engine plant. He told them that as long as he was the plant manager, there would be no layoffs—a comment that very probably would have gotten him fired if his boss had heard him say it. This statement alone gained Don a great deal of credibility with workers and their union leadership. It was the beginning of a truce that only got better with additional changes to enhance the working culture in the plant. These changes are listed in Table 23-1, on the following page.

CULTURAL CHANGES INITIATED AT THE TONAWANDA ENGINE PLANT

- Developing a passion for excellence in both product quality and work processes

- Encouraging employees to refer friends and relatives to buy GM cars through a sales relationship with a local car dealer

- Making work interesting through creative changes in work tasks and scope

- Eliminating bully management through training, retirements, and transfers

- Celebrating successes and holidays

- Cleaning up the plant and the landscaping of factory grounds

- Organizing a car show for the community on the factory grounds

- Making bottom-line profitability secondary to treating workers with respect and dignity

- Involving the workers (and UAW) in the decision-making process

- Creating a sense of pride in being employed at the Tonawanda Engine Plant

---

Table 23-1

The energy and spirits were running high at the plant as the culture changed. It came as no surprise that both workers and management decided to ignore the union contract for one day and pursue the world record in engine production. With two ten-hour shifts and the full cooperation of every plant employee, the Tonawanda Engine Plant established a world record that continues to go unchallenged today. This was a massive undertaking, and Don made it clear that it would not set a precedent for future production expectations but was to be used just to prove what a unified, focused, cooperative team could achieve. The pride that workers felt upon setting the world record was immense. You would have thought they had just won an Olympic gold medal. Employees at the plant drafted the public notice shown on the following page, "Thank You for Our Jobs," and donated the funds for the cost of publishing it.

SUSTAINABILITY OF CULTURE CHANGE

Is it possible for an organizational culture to maintain itself over time? To go through the immense effort and commitment of changing a culture only to see it revert to its former hostile, combative state would have been a tragedy. The question then becomes how GM could sustain this culture with changes in leadership in management, union, and workers. The answer is simple to articulate, yet it is difficult to accomplish.

THANK YOU For Our Jobs!

WE, THE EMPLOYEES OF CHEVROLET-PONTIAC-GM OF CANADA, TONAWANDA ENGINE PLANT, WOULD LIKE TO EXPRESS APPRECIATION TO OUR PLANT MANAGER, <u>DON RUST</u>, HIS STAFF, U.A.W. LOCAL #774 OFFICIALS AND OUR FELLOW HOURLY AND SALARIED EMPLOYEES.

WE, THE EMPLOYEES OF CPC TONAWANDA ENGINE HAVE PLEDGED TO FOLLOW THE PLANT MANAGER'S EXAMPLE IN THE MANUFACTURING OF A "WORLD CLASS" PRODUCT RIGHT HERE IN WESTERN NEW YORK. WE BELIEVE THAT THIS <u>COMMITMENT TO QUALITY</u> AND COMPETITIVENESS IN THE PRODUCTION OF OUR ENGINES IS THE ONLY WAY TO INSURE JOB SECURITY IN OUR AREA.

THROUGH THE DEDICATED EFFORTS OF THE ENTIRE ORGANIZATION, JOB OPPORTUNITIES FOR BOTH REPRESENTED AND SALARIED EMPLOYEES AT THE TONAWANDA ENGINE PLANT HAVE MULTIPLIED. A NEW PRIDE IN THE WORKPLACE AND IN OUR COMMUNITY HAS BEEN ESTABLISHED.

ONCE, AGAIN, THANK YOU MANAGEMENT, U.A.W. LOCAL #774, AND TO THE PEOPLE OF WESTERN NEW YORK; REST ASSURED WE ARE WORKING HARD TO PROMOTE CONTINUED AND INCREASED EMPLOYMENT IN OUR AREA. YOU CAN COUNT ON US!

EMPLOYEES

TONAWANDA ENGINE PLANT
CPC/GENERAL MOTORS CORP.
TONAWANDA, NEW YORK

Paid for by Employee Donations

191

The changes at the Tonawanda Engine Plant must be institutionalized, and traditions need to be established to continue the new culture. It has been twenty years since Don retired as plant manager. Four plant managers have been assigned to the plant over this time period. Not every one of these leaders embraced the changes that Don made. Some of the programs did not continue. Yet, a visit to the plant today would speak loudly for the fact that the energy and pride of the workers are still intact. Current leadership continues to invest in the culture of "Partners in Progress" that Don had created.

We believe that the positive energy in the plant, in itself, is a major reason why the culture has sustained itself. No rational leader would want to tamper with the productivity, commitment to quality, and energy of the workforce at this plant. While leaders may have their own way of doing things, the culture itself is embedded and seems to have developed internal resistance to go back to the days of industrial warfare. We might go so far as to claim that the organizational players know what other plants that have not gone through a dramatic change of culture are like and are loath to return to living their organizational lives in such a negative culture.

Twenty years after his retirement, workers still pay homage to their leader who made such a huge difference in their organizational lives.

HOW CAN GM LEVERAGE THE EXPERIENCE AT TONAWANDA?

What happened at the Tonawanda Engine Plant does not need to be a unique event. The principles that supported the changes there can be applied to other plants throughout the GM divisional structure. The changes described in this book are not difficult to understand. But, it will take leadership that believes in people and is willing to abandon the eighty-year history of warfare between management and the UAW to embrace a partnership that will change the work environment in the dozens of manufacturing plants in GM's organization. We believe the lessons learned from the Tonawanda Engine Plant can be the catalyst for change. We are hopeful that GM is listening and realizes how powerful an example they have available at the Tonawanda Engine Plant for creating the change that the current leadership of the company states it would like. We also believe the UAW leadership is ready to embrace this partnership that not only serves the needs of the company but also that of every worker who values working for a company that cares about them, respects them, and treats them with the dignity they deserve.

We believe that GM should be seeking leaders who embrace the values that Don brought to the company. These leaders must have a fundamental belief that workers deserve to be treated with trust, dignity, and respect. They must also be committed to changing the workplace to offer greater employment security for workers, more interesting work, support for a passion for excellence, more involvement in the business of not only making but helping to sell its products, and, most importantly, being on the same team in dealing with the competitive market forces that confront GM today.

We have told the story of how one plant of GM was able to change from a toxic, hostile culture to a positive culture embracing a partnership between management and worker to regain excellence and a high level of productivity. Now that the story is public, we hope that GM will seize the opportunity to leverage what happened at the Tonawanda Engine Plant to regain the stature it once had—and once again become the strongest automaker in the world.

EPILOGUE

Our advice to General Motors, in its quest to once again rise to a leadership role in the production of high-quality transportation products, is to call attention to how the Tonawanda Engine Plant engaged in a major change of its culture. Only when it engages in a corporate-wide culture change will GM recapture its greatness. We have described the heavy toll that industrial warfare and industrial depression had inflicted on all levels of GM management and its workforce. Without a major cultural change throughout the company, GM will continue to experience the trials and tribulations of industrial depression, challenges to quality, and financial stress.

It is our sincere hope that the future of GM will have a better outcome. In that spirit, we offer the following "nuggets" with the intention that they will inspire positive and lasting cultural change within GM.

1. If you are a business or a corporation, the men and women who make up your workforce are your most valuable asset.

2. If you are the top manager of a business or corporation and looking for continuous improvement from your workforce, try these three rules of engagement:
   a. Exhibit your faith in people
   b. Demonstrate your trust in them
   c. Show your respect for them

3. You should not expect a culture change in your business or corporation unless and until you have convinced your employees that you are leading by example.

4. A true culture change will, over time, be institutionalized in concert with the management style of its leaders.

5. Once you initiate a culture change, don't even think about turning back.

6. Human energy is not directly measurable, and it is released at the discretion of each individual.

7. Industrial depression will always be present in a toxic work culture, creating negative performance outcomes.

8. A bully manager will best serve in a management capacity somewhere outside your organization.

9. Workforce layoffs are inherently the result of poor planning.

10. A high quality of work life will only prevail in an atmosphere of real culture change.

11. Job security is the most important benefit any worker can receive.

12. Job security and workplace layoffs are incompatible.

13. The layoff problem must be solved before a true culture change can survive on a long-term basis.

14. A true culture change requires a positive relationship between management and workers.

15. Wasting human energy sets a terrible example.

16. It is long past the time for the eighty-year labor/management warfare to be replaced by a joint labor/management partnership.

17. Harmony in the workplace is a natural outcome to the adoption of a culture change in that workplace.

REFERENCES

Matrix at Michigan State University, "The Flint Sit-Down Strike Audio Gallery," n.d., http://flint.matrix.msu.edu/.

Ford, Henry, and Samuel Crowther. *My Life and Work*. Garden City, N.Y.: Garden City Publishing Co., 1922.

Gasson, Ruth. "Goals and Values of Farmers." *Journal of Agricultural Economics* 24, no. 3 (September 1973): 521-542.

Grodnitzky, Gustavo R. Culture Trumps Everything: *The Unexpected Truth about the Ways Environment Changes Biology, Psychology, and Behavior*. Newport, R.I.: Mountainfrog Publishing, 2014.

Hackett, Dewhurst. *Harley-Davidson: The Complete History*. London: Quarto Publishing Group, 2016.

Hackman, J. Richard, and Greg R. Oldham. *Work Redesign*. Reading, MA: Addison-Wesley, 1980.

"Lincoln Electric Company," n.d. Accessed at: www.referenceforbusiness.com/history2/98/Lincoln-Electric-Co.html

McGregor, Douglas. *The Human Side of Enterprise*. New York: McGraw-Hill, 1960.

"100 Best Companies to Work For." *Fortune*. February 6, 2012.

Sisodia, Rajendra, David B. Wolfe, and Jagdish N. Sheth. *Firms of Endearment: How World-Class Companies Profit from Passion and Purpose*. Second Edition. Upper Saddle River, N.J.: Pearson Education, 2014.

Taylor, Frederick Winslow. *The Principles of Scientific Management*. New York: Harper & Brothers, 1911.

Vance, J. D. *Hillbilly Elegy: A Memoir of a Family and Culture in Crisis*. New York: HarperCollins Publishers, 2016.

INDEX

INDEX

INDEX

INDEX

INDEX

ABOUT THE AUTHORS

DONALD L. RUST

was engaged in farming and military service throughout his first twenty-four years—along with a vision of becoming an aeronautical engineer. All of that ended abruptly when his boss at a Buick dealership encouraged him to enroll in an engineering program specializing in automobiles. Don received a scholarship to attend General Motors Institute, where he graduated with a degree in Industrial Engineering. Eager to have an impact on how cars and trucks were produced, he began his career at the Chevrolet engine plant in Flint, Michigan. He advanced through various levels of management that allowed him to observe an operating system he felt was severely flawed. Don witnessed the disdain that upper management exhibited for the organization's employees and the resistance those managers had toward any changes to the system proposed by lower-level managers. These observations motivated him to embark on a career-long commitment to making positive change in how employees are treated. The response to his efforts was so impressive that he accepted the challenge to create and sustain a culture change in all his future assignments. Don and his management team were able to turn the General Motors Tonawanda Engine Plant from being on the brink of closing to becoming one of the most efficient and productive engine plants in the world. Recognized for his achievements, Don received the Buffalo News Outstanding Citizen award in 1993. He has served on several boards, including the Federal Reserve Board of Buffalo, and the Board of International Motion Control Corporation. In his spare time, Don can be found in his wood studio making segmented bowls and vases of rare imported woods, and spending quality time with his family.

207

ALAN G. WEINSTEIN

has been a coach to CEOs, college professor, business consultant, author, and entrepreneur. He received his PhD in Industrial/Organizational Psychology from Wayne State University and has held professorships at Carnegie Mellon University, Oakland University, and Canisius College, where he was chair of the Management and Marketing Departments. At Canisius, Alan founded the Center for Entrepreneurship, the Institute for Family Business, and Entrepreneurs on Campus. With one of his students, he cofounded Lasertron, an Amherst, New York entertainment company that manufactures and operates laser tag court games. In 1992, Alan started the first TEC/Vistage group in upstate New York. He has served on several boards including Perry's Ice Cream, Lasertron, Stride Tool, and Ciminelli Development. Alan also facilitated a collaboration with several not-for-profit cultural organizations, helping them improve their financial health while allowing them to flourish artistically. He has won several awards for his work with entrepreneurs, including the Edwin A. Appel Award from Babson College. As a teacher, Alan was twice selected Outstanding Professor by Canisius College MBA students. His research has been published in several academic and professional journals, and for several years he coauthored a column titled "The Owner and Coach" in *Buffalo Business First*. His book, *Executive Coaching and the Process of Change*, was published in 2013. When not working, Alan can be found traveling, skiing, jogging, and working out at the gym, in order of enthusiasm.